SANCTIFICATION

SANCTIFICATION

Why We Resist God,
How to Overcome It

WILLIAM H. BAKER

Lamplighter Books Grand Rapids, Michigan
Zondervan Publishing House

SANCTIFICATION
Copyright © 1986 by William H. Baker

Lamplighter Books is an imprint of Zondervan Publishing House,
1415 Lake Drive, S.E., Grand Rapids, Michigan 49506.

Library of Congress Cataloging in Publication Data

Baker, William H., 1930–
  Sanctification : why we resist God, how to overcome it.

  Bibliography: p.
  1. Christian life. 2. Spiritual life. 3. Sanctification. I. Title.
BV4501.2.B3816 1986   234'.8   86-15983
ISBN 0-310-35301-7

Edited by Pamela M. Hartung

Printed in the United States of America

86 87 88 89 90 91 92 / 10 9 8 7 6 5 4 3 2 1

CONTENTS

Preface   7

CHAPTER ONE
Understanding the Problem:
Our Sinful Condition   9

The Place to Start
Defining Sin
Sin as Suppression
The Turning Point
The Downward Trend
Moralists and Religionists
The Necessary Remedy

CHAPTER TWO
The Solution: A Biblical Technique
for Dealing With Sin   33

The Logic of Romans 4–8
Affirming Our Relation to Christ
Affirming Christ's Lordship
The Need for Repentance
Paul Versus the Law
What We Must Admit
What We Must Allow

CHAPTER THREE
Implementing the Solution: The Great
Promoter   65

The Quiet, Powerful Spirit

The Arrival of the Spirit
The Spirit Convicts
The Spirit Intercedes
The Spirit Teaches
The Spirit Helps Us Interpret
The Spirit Enables
Natural and Spiritual

CHAPTER FOUR
Clarifying Basic Questions:
The Meaning of "Spirituality"   93

The Way We Used to Be
A Prevalent Misconception
Growing Without Pain
Growing in Trials
Growing Through Discipline
Growing Through Responsibility
Discipleship
Decision Making

CHAPTER FIVE
The Right Attitude: We're at War!   135

The Warfare Mentality
The Enemy Identified
Resisting and Standing
The Spiritual Resources

Appendix   161
Notes   173
Bibliography   187

Preface

You will never live a successful Christian life solely by reading a book on the subject. This book, however, can become a part of the process. It can provide an incentive that may lead you to live a vital Christian life. If it does, it will be because the Scripture passages found in this book will have become clearer to you. I have tried to let the Bible speak by looking at extended passages in their contexts and by digging into analysis of important words and verses.

Books like this one often present an author's unique methodology or approach, but too often such methodology is merely peppered with proof texts rather than with exegesis (the art of getting the meaning out of Scripture). The author's peculiar insight may be valuable, but the book lacks a thorough biblical viewpoint. You be the judge of whether I have succeeded where others have failed, but I have made an honest attempt to be faithful to Scripture.

The subject of this book merits several names: "*Christian life*," "*spiritual life*," and a more theological term, "*sanctification*." It can be treated in a narrow or broad sense. The narrow sense is restricted to spiritual exercises like Bible reading, prayer, and meditation; the broad perspective involves the total life. This book focuses on the broad perspective and has as its heart the biblical doctrine of sanctification—how we become more holy. Thus it is not a treatment of Christian ethics, involving individual issues of what is right or wrong behavior.

Let me give you an example. An important part of the spiritual life is prayer. You may be convinced that prayer is important, and you may desire to pray more. But if you are like me, you face a nagging problem. Prayer is hard work, or so it seems at times. In fact, at times prayer seems to be boring. Why is this? Well, ultimately it is due to some form of disobedience or indifference. Part of our problem, therefore, is to analyze human complacency and deal with it in connection with our prayer life. How is this done? It is done, first of all, by understanding more about what Scripture says about our relation to God. The problem of resistance to God permeates every area of life and stands in the way of every good thing we try to do.

Two things have aided me as I set out to write this book. The first is my own experience. My struggles and failures have driven me to interpret the Bible and seek its approach to the spiritual life. The second is that my position as a teacher allows me to bounce ideas off students who are willing to challenge me and drive me back to Scripture to refine my ideas through more careful exegesis.

Chapter One

Understanding

the Problem:

Our Sinful Condition

The Place to Start
Defining Sin
Sin as Suppression
The Turning Point
The Downward Trend
Moralists and Religionists
The Necessary Remedy

THE PLACE TO START

The starting point for living the spiritual life is not learning about the role of the Holy Spirit, the use of the Bible, or prayer. We must start by understanding ourselves.

To attempt to live the spiritual life without first understanding our basic condition is like trying to repair a car without knowing how it runs. You might be lucky and tighten a bolt, secure a spark-plug wire, or replace a broken fan belt. Sooner or later, however, you are going to face a breakdown that requires the services of someone who knows how the car runs. Likewise, you may get along in the spiritual life in a "hit-or-miss" method, but unless you understand what makes you "run," you will not make great progress.

The spiritual life is a constant encounter with our basic human tendency to resist God's will and do as we please. This is *sin*. We can use biblical techniques and resources to make an assault on this inclination, and in individual situations we can even defeat sin. But sin will never go away. This may be discouraging at first, but facing it and recognizing it is realistic. Any approach to the spiritual life that says you can apply some marvelous methodology and overcome your inclination toward sin in some final, absolute way is spiritual quackery.

But it is encouraging to know that with the help of the Holy Spirit, we can consistently do battle with sin. The true believer should *expect* to see progress, though at times it may be slow. The Bible wastes no time in introducing us to this truth. The first two chapters of Genesis describe how God created the universe and mankind. Genesis 3 explains the human condition. The first two human beings failed God's test of obedience by succumbing to a temptation to obtain something in a way contrary to God's provision. Essentially, it was an act of independence from God, hence an act of rebellion.

Adam's disobedience (he gets the primary blame because he acted in deliberate disobedience while Eve was deceived) infected the whole human race with a tendency to rebel against God. The apostle Paul explains this, "Therefore, just as through one man sin entered the world, and death through sin, and so death spread to all men, because all sinned . . . death reigned from Adam until Moses, even over those who had not sinned in the likeness of Adam's offense . . ." (Romans 5:12, 14). This was the historical beginning of our sinful condition. The rest of the Bible is the story of how God began and developed a process of dealing with the problems of our rebelliousness and how He restored us to a state of obedience.

Paul's letter to the Romans outlines the most penetrating analysis of the human condition. It sums up Old Testament material and concisely describes the actual effects Adam's fall had on his character and behavior. Furthermore, in the first eight chapters of Romans, Paul explains what God did to remedy this condition. We will survey these chapters to help us better understand our condition.

DEFINING SIN

Three words—sin, justification, and sanctification—serve as a simple outline of Romans 1–8. We cannot correctly understand ourselves until we understand what these three words mean.

If we are believers, we already have a basic understanding of these concepts, whether or not we are able to define them theologically. That's because we *had* to understand them in order to be saved; they contain the essential ideas of the gospel. Of course, whoever presented the gospel to us may not have used these actual words but others that we did understand. For example, some people who work in the evangelization of children use expressions like "wrong things" or "bad things" instead of "sins." This is because the word "sin" is not common to a child's everyday vocabulary.

In addition, even though we may be saved (true believers), we have a way of forgetting the process through which we came to saving faith. When I first applied for my present job, I was asked a lot of questions, and I asked a lot of questions, but I can't remember accurately everything we talked about. All I can remember for sure is that I was hired. Recently I had a good reason to wonder if something that my employer was requiring was clearly part of my original understanding of what the job entailed. This is why I consider it essential as a first step to go back to the basics, to clarify them and even increase our comprehension of them. This is, in fact, exactly what happens in the early part of Romans.

The first important word we need to understand is "sin." We often forget that sin involves our attitudes, not merely certain contemptible acts. Take stealing, for example. Not only is the stealing itself a sin, but the covetous attitude that may be behind this act is also sinful. And behind the covetousness lies a distrust in God's ability to provide all our needs. Romans 1:18–3:20 suggests this very idea—our fundamental problem is rooted in our attitude toward God.

A danger exists, however. We will see sin in some of its extreme forms of behavior, especially at the end of Romans 1, and we will be inclined to dismiss it as applying only to the most immoral pagans, not realizing that this is a description of the potential in all of us. The first group of people Paul describes are pagans who have no divine law or revelation from God. He then describes people who have a moral standard (and what is said about them could apply also to Jews). Finally, Paul explicitly addresses the Jews, who had the Holy Scriptures as a moral standard. These two latter groups would be like the pagans if they did not have a greater moral awareness because of the divine law. The first group, then, describes what we all would be like if God were not restraining our innate tendencies in one way or another.

What is sin? I prefer to answer that question with words that are simple yet theologically descriptive: "suppression of truth" or "rebellion against God." The first of these, "suppression," is found in Romans 1:18, and the other, "rebellion," sums up the conclusion found in Romans 3:10–18, though the word itself does not occur in the passage.

We often define sin in terms of various acts. We like to do this because it enables us to include in our idea of sin certain sins that we at present are not committing. Some Christians include on their lists of "sins" activities like movie attendance, smoking, drinking, and dancing while overlooking basic sins like selfishness, pride, and materialism.

Lists of sins, like the one in Romans 1:29–31, often occur in the Bible to remind the reader what sin *results* in. These are *sins*, but they are not *sin*. We need to get at the root of this matter because it will tell us—even believers—more about our basic nature.

SIN AS SUPPRESSION

The word "suppression" is the key term in Paul's description of the pagans who "suppress the truth in unrighteousness" (Rom. 1:18). "Suppress" is a translation of a Greek word that literally means "hold down." The truth gets held down or prevented from accomplishing anything. Furthermore, it is suppressed "in unrighteousness." "Righteousness" is the thematic word in Romans; it sums up our primary need in relation to God. And Romans tells how we receive it as a gracious provision of God. "Unrighteousness," therefore, sums up our problem. It is a summary of the sins cataloged in Romans 1:29–31: people are "filled with all unrighteousness." Probably "unrighteousness" is a synonym for "rebellion." This suppression occurs in a state of unrighteousness or rebellion. It is a constant tendency, the perversity of our nature.

This suppression takes many devious forms. I remember a man, for example, who held an inconsistent view about mankind's essential sinfulness. "Can you see the validity of the biblical truth that all people are prone to resist and disobey God?" I would ask.

"Oh, yes, I guess we all have a tendency to do that. I know human nature is rotten," he would respond.

Then at other times he would insist, "There are

people in this world who have never heard the message about Jesus Christ and who live very good lives. I just can't believe that God would send them to hell!"

Intellectually, he accepted the truth, but he could not allow that truth to seep down into his practical attitudes. Why? Probably because he still wanted to cling to human merit, especially his own. He had severe criticism for those who failed to meet his personal standards, which implied this self-righteous attitude. He knew the truth, but he suppressed it.

Romans 1:19–20 continues by explaining the kind of truth that is involved. The pagans have no Bible, but they nevertheless have truth. The "truth" that Paul describes is truth about God, not merely truth gained by scientific inquiry. At first, this is surprising. We who have been born and raised in a land where biblical truth is so available and where biblical morality has had such a profound influence (at least in the past) are inclined to think of the non-Christian areas of the world as totally ignorant about God. It is true that they must hear the gospel before they can be saved, as Romans 10:9–15 puts it:

> If you confess with your mouth Jesus as Lord, and believe in your heart that God raised Him from the dead, you shall be saved; for with the heart man believes, resulting in righteousness, and with the mouth he confesses, resulting in salvation. For the Scripture says, "Whoever believes in Him will not be disappointed." For there is no distinction between Jew and Greek; for the same Lord is Lord of all, abounding in riches for all who call upon Him; for "Whoever will call upon the name of the Lord will be saved." How then shall they call upon Him in whom they have not believed? And how shall they believe in Him whom they have not heard? And how shall they hear

without a preacher? And how shall they preach unless they are sent? Just as it is written, "How beautiful are the feet of those who bring glad tidings of good things!"

But this is not to say that they do not know something about God.

We have come to a profound concept of Romans, one that is not easily documented or proven from the way we all perceive our religious experience, but one that the authority of this letter demands we accept by faith. Paul suggests that the most devout and sincere followers of another religion really know better than to put their trust in any god other than the God of the Bible, who is revealed to them in their innermost being and in nature. They have turned away from some truth that they already had about God, that, if they had embraced it, would have led them toward the biblical Deity.

Ghandi, a dedicated non-Christian leader, exemplified some of the selflessness, courage, and commitment that the Bible commends to all true believers, yet he was not a believer in the New Testament sense of the term. His view of God was a mixture of Christian, Muslim, and primarily Hindu concepts. "There was a time," Ghandi once wrote, "when I was wavering between Hinduism and Christianity. When I recovered my balance of mind, I felt that to me salvation was possible only through the Hindu religion, and my faith in Hinduism grew deeper and more enlightened."[1]

Here was a man who knew much biblical truth. He admired Jesus Christ but ignored much of what Jesus had to say about God, mankind, and salvation. Such arbitrary picking and choosing is an outstanding example of the universal tendency to suppress the truth and still emerge as a dedicated, admired religious figure.

Why don't we readily acknowledge this turning away if it is true? Precisely because of our tendency to suppress the truth in unrighteousness! Is this talking in circles? No, because it is observable to those willing to see it, to those who are no longer blind.

The apostle Paul, who writes under inspiration, confidently asserts that this truth about God is "evident" to them (Rom. 1:19). He means that through the material universe that cries out for an explanation, a person should reach the conclusion that there is a Being of "eternal power and divine nature" behind it all (Rom. 1:20).

I don't believe that this is exactly the same as mere belief in a god; many believe in a god who does not respond to the implications of such a truth, or they believe in a god of their own making. They do not "honor Him as God, or give thanks" (Rom. 1:21). Thus a claim to believe in a god does not qualify as a response to this truth that is evident to all. Ironically, religion made by the human mind is merely a pious (I avoid the term "sincere") form of suppression of true religion.

To complete this picture of our understanding of God, Romans 2:14–15 teaches that in addition to the "revelation" in nature, we also have a kind of witness to truth *within* us. It is a sort of "law" that takes the place of the written law. A person's conscience tells him or her what is right or wrong, but that conscience may not always be accurate in relation to God's law. This makes no difference because the words "these . . . are a law to themselves" (Rom. 2:14) and "their thoughts alternately accusing or else defending them" (Rom. 2:15) imply that God considers it sufficient basis for judging them; they do not always obey even this less precise sense of right and wrong.

18

Understanding the Problem

Even people in remote, unaffected areas of the world can be righteously judged on the basis of their response to what they already know both about God and about morals. This same passage, however, is not encouraging about whether anyone is likely to respond righteously to such revelation, at least apart from any prodding from God (theologians call this "prevenient grace"). I say this for two reasons: first, we have already seen that people suppress the truth deliberately. Second, Romans 3:10–11 seems to be categorical: no one is righteous, and no one seeks after God.

On the other hand, Romans 10 strongly implies that anyone who wants to call on the name of the Lord will receive the necessary message in order to do so. My conclusion is that when a rebellious person seeks the Lord, God is working in that person to do whatever is necessary to alter the innate tendency to suppress truth so that the person will seek and believe the gospel.

A good example of this is found in Acts 10. Cornelius was a "devout man, and one who feared God" (Acts 10:2). He attended the Jewish synagogue (the implication of the technical expression "one who feared God") and evidently had been attracted to the biblical God. We could speculate that stage by stage he had come that far, a little more light added to the light he already had. Something was overcoming his natural tendency to suppress the truth. He had reached the place for further truth to be added so that he could be brought to the threshold of salvation itself.

In order for this to happen, God prepared a messenger, Peter, not an easy task in itself due to Peter's inherited prejudices against Gentiles. Besides this, Cornelius himself is further prepared by a vision that leads him to send a trusted messenger to fetch the apostle Peter.

The grand finale occurs when Peter enters the Roman soldier's home and presents the good news about Jesus Christ. Indeed, it seems that God has committed Himself to get the truth about Christ to anyone who is disposed to believe it.

THE TURNING POINT

We have seen how people deliberately and maliciously turn away from truth that is plain to them. How they do this and the immediate and eventual consequences of this action also help us understand the meaning of sin. Romans 1:21 shows us just where the turning point occurs: "For even though they knew God, they did not honor Him as God, or give thanks." From this point a moral and spiritual decline sets in. First, false religion or idolatry takes the place of the true knowledge of God (Rom. 1:22–23); next, the first in a series of expressions, "God gave them over" (Rom. 1:24–25), describes the decline from immorality to sexual perversion (Rom. 1:26–27) and finally to a "depraved mind" (Rom. 1:28–32).

This sounds like a "domino" theory of sin, doesn't it? One thing topples over only to strike another and so on. This is why we should be so concerned when we see sin in its earliest stages; something worse will follow if we allow sin to go unchecked. If this is so, then it is extremely important to detect the earliest stage of the falling dominoes, the first one, in fact, so that the process may never begin.

This turning point, described in verse 21, is interesting and significant. Mankind "knew" God but failed to honor Him as God and give Him thanks. This original state would have been unique for Adam and Eve, for no one would have known God as they had. But this statement about knowing God refers more to mankind as a whole. It means that in some secondary sense, all people "know" God; earlier in this passage Paul says that people have suppressed the truth evident to them (Rom. 1:18). In concrete terms it means that every human being comes to a point in life where he or she acts decisively upon a knowledge of God that is true so far as it goes. Looking at the world as a whole, the person acts to reject this knowledge and opt for something else instead. As human constructions of religion developed and became more widely accepted, whatever kind they might be, people would have tended to follow them because their parents, relatives, and friends believed these religions.

This is a religious history of each of us, though it unfolds somewhat differently for each of us. Take, for example, how it would work out in a Christian society like ours. Biblical truth about God is relatively prevalent in our society. A lot of people think of themselves as Christians but are far from it in strictly biblical terms. They believe something that resembles biblical Christianity, but at some point their minds deliberately have perverted a crucial aspect of it. The most likely aspect they might pervert or ignore is the truth of the perfect moral purity ("holiness") of God and its demand upon them to live a morally pure life. They like the idea of God's love, and the idea of God's greatness satisfies them intellectually. "Love," of course, means to them that God is always forgiving or indifferent to what His Word says is right and wrong. This is not the God of the Bible, but a "do-it-yourself" god, created for the sake of convenience.

Whatever form this turning point takes, it amounts to not honoring God or giving thanks. The religious history described in Romans 1 can also describe a society's religious and moral decline, which can then lead to the decline of whole civilizations. Romans 1 is saying that it all begins as a decline in a person's understanding of God.

Failing to worship God ("not honoring or being thankful") precipitates the "turning point." This makes worship a vital occupation. Some of you may have thought about worship as merely reciting a formal liturgy that you do not understand or going to church Sunday morning out of a sense of duty. But worship is a life-involving activity of recognizing God for who He is.

Failure to worship God, failure to appreciate Him for who He is, is the turning point in one's relationship to God. Believers readily acknowledge this. Worship involves what is important in our lives, and true worship, therefore, is putting God first in everything. This idea is behind Israel's famous "Shema" in Deuteronomy 6:4–5: "Hear, O Israel! The LORD is our God, the LORD is one! And you shall love the LORD your God with all your heart and with all your soul and with all your might." Jesus regarded this as the greatest commandment (Matt. 22:37) because putting God first in this way was the key to keeping all the other commandments (Matt. 22:40).

We are creatures of some form of worship; that is, something takes priority in our lives. It may be money, art, sex, material things, or whatever, but something is first in every person's life. As an illustration, look at something that is worthwhile and beautiful in itself: art. An art lover, like the devotee to anything, *lives* art. Even if this person's occupation is not related to art, he or she may endure work just to be able to spend time viewing or collecting masterpieces. Leisure time is spent reading about art; or if the person also has artistic talent, he or she may spend time painting or whatever. The art lover's friends are likely to be people who share the same interests. Art becomes a kind of religion. The person is indifferent to God—often feeling indifferent even to formal religion as something unnecessary in his or her life. Until something starts going wrong.

The lesson is this: if we don't worship God, we will worship something else. But God will not tolerate this, for He is a "jealous" God (Exod. 20:5), not in a selfish sense but in a very *un*selfish sense because He knows that the worship of anything but Him will destroy our souls. He made us for Himself. He will not "tolerate" idolatry in the believer and will thus discipline the believer in some way to correct this sin (Heb. 12:5–13).

God will not tolerate idolatry in mankind as a whole. Romans 1 describes the consequences of this initial sin of all sins. Three times Paul says that "God gave them over" (Rom. 1:24, 26, and 28). For the sake of convenience, I will call this "judicial abandonment" by God. It is judicial in the sense that it is just or fitting, and it is an abandonment because God does not punish in a direct way but simply lets people carry out the natural consequences of what they are doing. Sin always hurts a person, if not immediately, at least ultimately, because it usually involves some physiological or psychological harm. Each of these judicial abandonments leads to a condition worse than the others.

THE DOWNWARD TREND

Undoubtedly some people would dispute the claim that the homosexuality described in Romans 1:26–27 is a worse condition than the other forms of immorality described in Romans 1:24. But this passage as a whole describes situations that go from bad to worse; certainly no one can dispute the fact that the last of these three abandonments results in man at his worst.

You may wonder how I can take a passage that clearly pertains to the unregenerate pagan and apply it to the believer. I do this on the basis of what is said in Romans 6, that something of the old unregenerated person continues to persist in us even now as regenerated believers. My logic is simply this: we can learn about a part of who we are now from looking at what we used to be totally. Thus Romans 1:18–3:19 describes the sinful tendency in every believer. If we understand the person we were, the "old self," we can better understand that part of us that still rebels against God.

Paul describes some things in this downward trend that could probably never happen to a regenerated believer because of the resources God has given to the believer. For example, God disciplines His own and sends the Holy Spirit to live in the believer to prod him or her to a pure life in various ways. It is doubtful, therefore, that God would permit the believer to decline to the point of the second stage of God's "giving over," sexual perversion, unless the believer perhaps had been a homosexual before becoming a Christian. But some items in Paul's list of sins in Romans 1:29–31 can and do temporarily express themselves in the believer's life. Hate can occur in my reaction to something someone does to me, and this is tantamount to murder (see Matt. 5:21–26). A Christian might be disobedient to a parent on occasion. The final verses of Romans 1 describe a stage of depravity in which all or many of these sins *characterize* a person. The true believer should be characterized by obedience to God, though he or she could occasionally commit any one of these sins.

The lesson thus far is this: believers are still capable of a relapse into the old ways. This relapse begins when we fail to worship God, when something other than God becomes more important to us. This "idolatry" can lead to a temporary hardness and loss of restraint, and we soon will find ourselves back in sinful practices and attitudes.

Another danger exists. After we have been believers for some time, a moral conditioning takes place that causes us to commit sin in less obvious ways. We may even reach a plateau where immorality is remote and habits of self-control have made us less conscious of the subtle ways we can sin. For example, take the case of "vicarious sinning" that is so common today. We are able to sit in front of the television set and gratify ourselves through the immoral acts of the players. An otherwise unobjectional and moral hero or heroine can suddenly commit fornication, and we find ourselves excusing them for it because we have identified with them in some way in the course of the story. Romans 1:32 describes this as giving "hearty approval" to those who actually practice the sin while not actually doing it ourselves because of our built-in moral restraints. For this reason, it is important for us to look at Romans 2 (describing the Jew's sin—the sin of one who has the Bible).

MORALISTS AND RELIGIONISTS

Paul addresses a different kind of person at the beginning of Romans 2: the person "who passes judgment" on someone else. Let's call these people the "moralists," for they are critical of others' moral behavior. Later, in verse 17, Paul addresses the Jew by name, although admittedly what he says about the moralist he also could say about the Jew. I am inclined to think that Paul has the Gentile in mind because he describes such a person in verses 14–15: "For when Gentiles who do not have the Law do instinctively the things of the Law, these, not having the Law, are a law to themselves, in that they show the work of the Law written in their hearts, their conscience bearing witness, and their thoughts alternately accusing or else defending them."

It is easy for us as believers to detect some similarities between ourselves and these two groups, especially the Jews. It is interesting to see how each class of humanity reacts to the truth it has. Some kind of suppression takes place.

No time is wasted in getting to the heart of the moralists' suppression: "Therefore you are without excuse, every man of you who passes judgment, for in that you judge another, you condemn yourself; for you who judge practice the same things" (Rom. 2:1). Evidently, the moralists' morality or sense of justice exists solely for their own benefit. They seem to practice it as much for the purpose of judging and looking down upon others as for a way of life and conviction of right and wrong.

The moralists fail to judge themselves; hence they suppress the truth. They consider themselves a cut above most others because they do a better job of practicing right and wrong. They may admit that they are not perfect, but they are likely to blame their failures on their humanity. Many moralists are blind to their faults, having defined sin in such a way that they never do it.

The indictment of Romans 2 is much more severe than to let any of these excuses get by. "Not the hearers of the Law are just before God, but the doers of the Law will be justified" (Rom. 2:13) are words that require genuine, consistent righteousness, not merely a hard try. This does not mean that anyone will be justified by keeping the law. It suggests an impossible standard that God will accept. And it means that the "doers of the Law" are those people who are justified by faith and who succeed in doing the law only because of God's grace. "Doing the Law" is more than good morals and good works; it involves real obedience undergirded by an attitude of love for God.

But moralists are far from being perfect morally. Romans 2:15 implies that moralists alternately accuse and defend themselves; they break their own rules and their consciences tell them so. Through this, God is telling them to admit their sin and repent (Rom. 2:4–5).

What does this mean to us? We have a tendency to consider partial obedience to moral standards as good enough, and we are lenient with ourselves. Repeated often enough, this makes us self-righteous and blind to our faults—danger signals to our waywardness toward God. The solution is not stricter outward obedience but repentance. This repentance then allows God to work within us a more consistent righteousness.

Paul accuses the Jews of essentially the same thing, but this accusation has a fascinating twist to it. Romans 2:17–29 describes the Jews as people who consider themselves to be superior because they have knowledge of God's explicit will in the Scriptures. They regard themselves as "a corrector of the foolish, a teacher of the immature" (Rom. 2:20). But Jews, too, fail to keep this higher standard; mere knowledge and agreement with its truth are not sufficient to produce consistently obedient behavior. The interesting "twist," however, is that Jews may not necessarily break the rules they preach and teach in precisely the same way as those to whom they consider themselves superior. They do not worship the same idols, but they rob temples (Rom. 2:22). They worship the money that constitutes the value of the gold idol. The Jews commit *equivalent* sins. They define what sin is in terms of certain obvious things and mark them off as things they will not do. Usually the forbidden actions are things that they are not tempted to do anyway. Idolatry can involve many things, but the Jews arbitrarily limit it to just a few. They limit sin to specific deeds instead of attitudes.

The Jews, then, do not obey God from a heart of love. They are Jews "outwardly" but not "inwardly" (Rom. 2:28–29).

In addition to this subtle form of hypocrisy, the Jews were victims of yet another delusion. Several key words in this passage reveal it: they "relied" on the law (2:17); they "approved" the law; they were "confident" in their position; they "abhorred" idols; they "boasted" in the law (2:23). These words reveal a double standard in which the Jews thought that as long as they agreed with God's standards, giving mental assent to them, their very agreement carried with it a kind of righteousness, regardless of whether they actually kept the law.

Now let's see how relevant this description of the law is to modern Evangelicalism. We Evangelicals are susceptible to very similar errors, first of all, in legalistically making our lists of forbidden practices yet failing to recognize equivalents elsewhere in our behavior. For example, some Evangelicals prohibit their constituents from patronizing commercial movie theaters but indiscriminately watch similar, if not identical movies on the television. I do not criticize the practice of not attending the theater; I criticize our inconsistency.

Secondly, we as Evangelicals often fall into the trap of

giving lip service to truth without incorporating it into our lives, imagining that our agreement with the church's doctrinal statement makes us "orthodox" or "fundamental." Like the Jews, we delude ourselves into a false sense of security by thinking of ourselves as God's chosen people merely because we subscribe to orthodox doctrine. This gets so extreme that we isolate ourselves in our Christian circles and activities, and we are then unable to evangelize others effectively.

For example, have you ever noticed how few of the "ministries" of the church actually serve the community around us? How well do most of us know our neighbors, the ones we're supposed to be reaching with the truth?

These are ways we suppress the truth by selfish, self-centered living. In it all we maintain a facade of Christianity and "churchianity." Is it any wonder that although we are counted in the millions by the Gallup poll, we are making little impact on the society around us?

THE NECESSARY REMEDY

Now we can understand the basic truth of the spiritual life and sanctification: if any progress is to be made in our lives, God must do it. Yet this is not to say that we are to be passive; as a matter of fact, we need to be tremendously active. We must *let* God work in us—the secret of the spiritual life. Our resistance is the major barrier against our spiritual growth. Equally true is the paradox that God Himself works in us to bring about our willingness to let Him work.

Once we have come to understand our sin, we must come to understand "justification" and "sanctification." We have seen how the pagan, the moralist, and the Jew suppressed the truth, and this has helped us understand the insidious nature of sin. We're ready to see how God remedies our sin through justification and sanctification.

We must also understand how "grace" is related to both justification and sanctification. Justification is by grace (Rom. 3:24), and the complete formula is that we are saved "by grace ... through faith" (Eph. 2:8). Sanctification, too, is accomplished by grace, although both words, so far as I know, do not occur together. Yet the idea is taught in the Bible, for the believer's whole life is lived by faith in God's ability to work in and through him or her, and this is grace. Grace is simply God doing for us what we cannot do for ourselves.

God has to provide justification and sanctification by grace as the remedy for sin because our bondage in sin makes it impossible for us to save ourselves. I personally view the problem more specifically as our *unwillingness* to do anything to save ourselves, especially in regard to coming to faith in Christ.[1] We have already seen how we rebel against God. There are no people who want to be saved but who just cannot be saved. If I said that we *cannot* save ourselves, this might be understood as an unfortunate circumstance. But we are not mere victims of circumstances—we deliberately stray from God. We must blame only ourselves for our spiritual failures.

Due to the limited scope of this book, we cannot deal extensively with justification. Justification, to define it briefly, is a legal concept meaning "to declare someone righteous in God's sight because of faith, even though the person is still a sinner in practice." This means that we are *simultaneously* righteous as well as sinners. We are "righteous" in the sense that Christ's death has satisfied God's law by paying the price of our guilt. We have put our trust in Christ's payment, and we have been justified—pronounced "not guilty." It would be incorrect, therefore, to say "I am *made* righteous," for this would imply that I have always behaved that way.

Sanctification picks up where justification leaves off. Since I was also "regenerated" by the Holy Spirit (John 3:5) when I was justified, I have a new desire to obey God, a desire I lacked before. Sanctification makes righteousness a part of my behavior or practice, whereas justification made it a matter of my standing before God. Literally, the word *sanctify* means "to make holy." God's remedy for our condition is the only way we can be helped: we must allow Him to work both in and through us.

Chapter Two

The

Solution:

A Biblical Technique for Dealing With Sin

The Logic of Romans 4–8
Affirming Our Relation to
   Christ
Affirming Christ's Lordship
The Need for Repentance
Paul Versus the Law
What We Must Admit
What We Must Allow

THE LOGIC OF ROMANS 4–8

What our faith has accomplished legally (Romans 4–5) must take place in our lives practically (Romans 6–8). God gives us the righteousness that grants us this right standing with Him, but righteousness also must become a part of our everyday living. Several key words help to clarify this truth:

Romans 4–5	Romans 6–8
Our position	Our practice
Our standing	Our state

I see a logical three-step progression in Romans 6, 7, and 8, with each step related roughly to one of the chapters. Charted, they look like this:

Romans 6	Romans 7	Romans 8
What we must *affirm*	*admit*	*allow*

First, we must affirm two basic truths about our relation to Jesus Christ. Then we must admit a fact about ourselves in connection with sin. Finally, we must allow certain activities of the Holy Spirit. We may not always be fully conscious of these steps in our own experience, but to some degree they must take place whenever we deal effectively with sin.

The way we think determines the way we act. Jesus taught, for example, that lust leads to adultery (Matt. 5:28), that hate leads to murder (Matt. 5:21–22). Proverbs 23:7

35

says that as a person "thinks within himself, so he is." Likewise, our attitude toward sin will determine to some extent what we do about it. There is a limit to this, however, when we consider the sin nature. Good thoughts do not always produce good actions. If this were true, it would simplify the Christian life, and I suppose we all would be perfect in our behavior in a matter of days or weeks.

But attitudes *are* important. Romans 6 tells us how to deal with our sinful attitudes. Note how Romans 6:3 and 6:16 begin: "Do you not *know?*" (italics added). In other words, based upon something Christ has done, we should think about sin a certain way. Each of these rhetorical questions answers another question asked by an imaginary person who misunderstands something radical that has been said.

For example, Romans 5:20–21 contains this unusual statement about God's grace: ". . . where sin increased, grace abounded all the more." This is a paradox, which is followed with the cynical question, "Are we to continue in sin that grace might increase?" (Rom. 6:1). Such a question, of course, totally overlooks the purpose of salvation, that our lives might glorify God.

A few verses later, Paul makes another striking statement: ". . . you are not under the law, but under grace" (Rom. 6:14). In other words, we no longer live under the condemnation of the law but under the forgiveness and provision of God's grace. The cynic again retorts, "Shall we sin because we are not under law, but under grace?" (Rom. 6:15). The answer follows: "Do you not know that when you present yourselves to someone as slaves for obedience, you are slaves of the one whom you obey. . . ?" (Rom. 6:16).

The Solution

I once worked at a job I hated. I had to rise very early in the morning, work hard all day, and frequently confront other workers who failed to do their own jobs well—a task that was contrary to my easy-going nature. Finally, I left this unpleasant job and took another that I thoroughly enjoyed. Was I now free from getting up early, working hard all day, and confronting people about their shortcomings? No! I had merely switched my allegiance to another "boss." You see, I had entered the ministry.

So we, in a similar fashion, having left the slavery of Satan's oppression due to the broken law, have entered a new and delightful servitude to Jesus Christ where the demands are equally strict but our reasons for obeying are pleasant.

These two rhetorical questions confront us with two things that we must with all our hearts affirm: the implications of our baptism and the rights of our new Master over us.

AFFIRMING OUR RELATION TO CHRIST

Romans 6 begins with a question. Paul asks if his readers realize an important truth that another question, "Shall we sin that grace may increase?" seems to overlook. This truth involves the believer's relation to Jesus' death, burial, and resurrection, and the relationship is expressed with the word "baptized." When each believer was baptized "into" Christ, he or she was baptized into Jesus' death, burial, and resurrection. Whether this baptism should be understood as the ordinance of water baptism or Spirit baptism (1 Cor. 12:13) is not important to our point. The important point is that at some definite time in the past each believer came to be related in some way to the death, burial, and resurrection of Jesus Christ. It must be some sort of theoretical relationship—perhaps "theological" is a better term—because no one is actually crucified with Christ.

When we put our faith in Jesus Christ, God looks at us in a new way. We are legally joined to Christ's death and resurrection, as if we ourselves had been there and it had happened to us.

Let's think of this by imagining what a first-century Christian may have been thinking as he got baptized:

> What a day this is! I have heard this amazing news that Jesus the Nazarene, God's only Son, willingly went to His death on a cross, was buried, and rose again from the dead to satisfy the requirements of the divine law on my behalf and to prove that God accepted it. I'm going to show this before my friends and fellow believers—even if it means that my old friends will reject or persecute me. I'm going to confess Jesus as Lord and promise to trust and follow Him. I don't take this lightly because it will force me to put my inner conviction to the test. I am crossing over the line, not only inwardly but outwardly, and I will never be the same again!

Baptism, like a marriage ceremony, is a legally binding public commitment. Baptismal vows, like marriage vows, are a public promise to trust in and follow someone—in this case, Jesus Christ. Each, then, marks a turning point in a person's life. Our thinking about ourselves must be different after this turning point. The married person's thinking and decisions will take his or her beloved mate into account, and the person will never be independent again. Likewise, believers must think about themselves— and Jesus Christ—quite differently after baptism (or conversion, if you prefer).[1] Romans 6:2 calls this radical change of thinking a "death" to sin. This death means new life: "For if we have become united with Him in the likeness of His death, certainly we shall be also in the likeness of His resurrection. . ." (Rom. 6:5).

The person we were before our baptism is called "the old self" (lit., "the old man"). The opposite of the "old self" is the "new self," the person we have now become.[2] The "old self" was "crucified" with Christ and should be regarded as "dead." The crucifixion of the old self takes place, according to Romans 6:6, so that the "body of sin" (a figure of speech for those times during which our body is controlled by sin) might cease. This unusual expression, "body of sin," seems to be a vivid way of describing the dominion that sin has over the body or total person during times of a person's disobedience to God's commandments. Thus it is a rough equivalent of the word "flesh," or what some theologians call the "sin nature."

Our commitment to Christ, expressed outwardly by baptism, brings about this death of the "old self," a passing from one life or realm to another in which sin has no legal right to control us. This idea will be developed starting with Romans 6:12.

How does this affect us? Does something automatically occur merely because we become Christians? No. Instead, this is where "right thinking" or "affirming" comes in, and this is what Romans 6:11 is saying: "Even so *consider* yourselves to be dead to sin, but alive to God in Christ Jesus" (italics added). Let's return to the previous illustration. A newly married person "considers" himself or herself to be married whenever the impulse to flirt with another person occurs. By way of analogy, we attempt to stifle unfaithfulness to our Lord by *considering* or *affirming* ourselves to be "dead" to some selfish impulse, recognizing it as part of the "old self." We then vow to live "resurrection life" and be obedient to our baptism. This requires a new frame of mind, a difficult, radical mindset. Why would we want to think in a way that often forces us to deny ourselves something? Because we know that it will lead to something better, even though we are denying ourselves something that seems attractive.

I'll admit that from the human standpoint the acquiring of this new frame of mind is formidable. This is true because the sin nature is still active *until* it has been dealt with in this manner (more about this later). The work of the Holy Spirit is necessary to prod us to such difficult decisions.

To summarize, then, resisting sin begins with a way of *thinking*. We must see ourselves as God sees us: crucified, buried, and risen again with Jesus Christ. We are new people who have entered upon a new life during which many things incompatible with this new life keep confronting us for decision, a decision in which we renounce the "unfruitful deeds of darkness" (Eph. 5:11) by affirming ourselves, indeed, to be dead to sin.

One word of caution before we move on. The expression "dead to sin" does not mean that we are immune to temptation as a corpse is immune to all physical stimuli. This implies indifference toward sin. Even if one were to theorize such a possibility during brief periods of time, it would be misleading and unrealistic. Both experience and Scripture testify that sin continues within us: "If we say that we have no sin, we are deceiving ourselves, and the truth is not in us" (1 John 1:8). Another clue that this is not what "dead to sin" means is the use of the same expression with regard to Christ Himself. Romans 6:10 says that Christ also "died to sin." Though the phrase means something different in His case, it certainly cannot mean immunity to temptation to sin, for although Christ was tempted, He never sinned, and He cannot be described as having passed from sin. What it may mean is that when He died, He passed from sin's power and effects that He experienced in His physical sufferings and abuse by sinful people.

AFFIRMING CHRIST'S LORDSHIP

In addition to affirming our baptism, we must affirm that we are no longer slaves to sin but rather to righteousness, which means a recognition of the lordship of Christ. Paul develops the idea of verse 6 by elaborating on the metaphor of the master and the slave (Rom. 6:12–23). Death to sin is a termination of servitude to sin, but the possibility of sin's enslaving us continues to exist, at least to a degree. Our experience differs from God's perspective until we make our experience conform with God's perspective.

We have a new Master, but the old master doesn't seem to recognize the new Master's right to be in control. It is as if the old master keeps returning to put us to work again for him, forcing us to tell him to go away.

We see two important principles in this section of Romans. First, we have only two choices available to us when we face a moral decision: we can be slaves to sin or "slaves to righteousness." "Slavery to righteousness" (Rom. 6:19) is ironic language because it actually is a kind of freedom. We might imagine that some other alternative such as doing as we please without necessarily sinning is open to us, but it really is not. Anything but biblical righteousness is actually a form of rebellion against God and therefore is sin. There is no such thing as freedom apart from God. The question of the spiritual life is "to whom will I be wholly devoted?" We can choose between two masters; that's all.

If we think about the consequences of doing only as we please, then we can see how this works. Self-denial requires self-discipline, but self-indulgence leads to more and more desire and less and less satisfaction. Soon we find ourselves in a merry-go-round of looking for new ways to satisfy our cravings, and we eventually wake up to the frustrating realization that we are slaves, out of control and miserable.

Why does Paul use the ironic term "slavery" to describe the other alternative, righteousness? Aren't believers "free" (Gal. 5:1)? Yes we are, but our freedom involves an "obedience" (Rom. 6:16–17). Paradoxically, however, this is a pleasant experience. Slavery to sin leads finally to death (Rom. 6:16, 21), but slavery to righteousness leads to eternal life (Rom. 6:22) and sanctification (Rom. 6:19). This kind of "slavery" is freedom! When we come into harmony with the Creator of the universe, we are free. Some of the irony in the use of the term "slaves to righteousness" may be due to our warped perspective, which makes submitting to righteousness appear to be unpleasant, until we have actually done it. This is what makes obedience to God so difficult. Sin has an allurement that gives righteousness the illusion of unpleasantness.

Let me illustrate the reason why obedience to God, slavery to righteousness, can rightly be called "freedom." Since obedience to God is the purpose for which He created us, we perform the best in such obedience and malfunction in any other kind of control (or lack of it). A

The Solution

new automobile (with a few exceptions due to lack of quality control) performs the way its designers intended. These designer intentions obviously require a driver to be in control. As I, the driver, operate it properly, the car responds the way it is supposed to. As it gradually receives wear and neglect, it ceases to perform according to the maker's specifications. In a manner of speaking, it ceases to be "free" to perform as it should. If the car had feelings of its own, I'm sure it would not feel free and would long to be restored by repair to its original capabilities. I'd like to think my car prefers to be obedient to my intentions as its driver.

Obedience to God is our destiny, that for which we were created. Our greatest happiness and fulfillment will be found in honoring our Creator through righteousness.

Another important principle in Romans 6:12–7:6 is sin's unrelenting nature to dominate if the believer does not deal with it decisively. This is seen in the forms of the verb "to present" in verse 13. The word itself means "to make something fully available for use." We make our bodies (that includes all of us as persons) available either for sin or for righteousness. We decide to do this, although in the case of sin, we may be less aware of it sometimes as we sort of "fall" into it. The verb tenses are unique to the Greek language in that they do not express time as they do in English. The New American Standard version makes an attempt at conveying the meaning of the Greek when it translates the first "present" as "do not go on presenting the members of your body to sin." Although the tense of this "present" is the Greek present, which does not always imply continuous or habitual activity, in this case, due to the contrast being made by the next "present" in the Greek aorist, it probably does imply such habitual action.

The second "present," translated merely as "present yourselves to God," needs to be rendered with more precision to do justice to the fact that its tense is different. Paul must have had a deliberate reason for this. I believe he was trying to show how different sinning was from doing right. Normally the Greek tense used for presenting oneself to righteousness is ambiguous, but the most reliable Greek authorities conclude that Paul implies here a decisive act. Thus the best translation, though cumbersome, would be: "present yourself with great resolve to God."

Some interpreters erroneously translate "present yourselves to God" as a "once-for-all" type of action and build a concept of a major dedicatory event, that radically changes one's course of life. Most grammarians, however, do not support such a view of this verb tense.[3] Neither is such a concept supported by the experience of most believers, who never reach such a plateau in their spiritual lives, but continue day by day to deal with the efforts of sin to overtake them, though the "sin" may be in the form of selfishness, complacency, and resentment rather than gross immorality.

The romanticizing of certain spiritual crises in the lives of famous people has contributed to this misleading concept. D. L. Moody had a very profound experience that some biographers have labeled as a "second work of grace," and it had a continuing effect upon his life and ministry. But this does not make such an experience the norm for all believers. And we should not look upon such an experience, real as it was for Moody, as a shortcut to spiritual power for ourselves, too. It was no shortcut for Moody.

The apostle Paul's testimony in Philippians 3:8–16

provides insight into this issue. As you read this, think about whether Paul suggests that his life was determined by some major dedicatory event.

> I count all things to be loss in view of the surpassing value of knowing Christ Jesus my Lord, for whom I have suffered the loss of all things, and count them but rubbish in order that I may gain Christ, and may be found in Him, not having a righteousness of my own derived from the Law, but that which is through faith in Christ, the righteousness which comes from God on the basis of faith, that I may know Him, and the power of His resurrection and the fellowship of His sufferings, being conformed to His death; in order that I may attain to the resurrection from the dead. Not that I have already obtained it, or have already become perfect, but I press on in order that I may lay hold of that for which also I was laid hold of by Christ Jesus. Brethren, I do not regard myself as having laid hold of it yet; but one thing I do: forgetting what lies behind and reaching forward to what lies ahead, I press on toward the goal for the prize of the upward call of God in Christ Jesus. Let us therefore, as many as are perfect, have this attitude; and if in anything you have a different attitude, God will reveal that also to you; however, let us keep living by that same standard to which we have attained.

Spiritual goals are a matter of continual, day-by-day decisions. To "keep living by that same standard to which we have attained" is to keep living by the same faith that brought us into our present relationship to God. I do not find that Scripture teaches some massive, life-changing dedicatory event as the norm for all believers.

What's the point of it all? The point is that sinning is a relative matter of habit and decisions to present ourselves to sin relatively unconscious acts of the will, but doing

Sanctification

Fig. 1

VIEWS OF LORDSHIP
"Lordship Salvation" theory

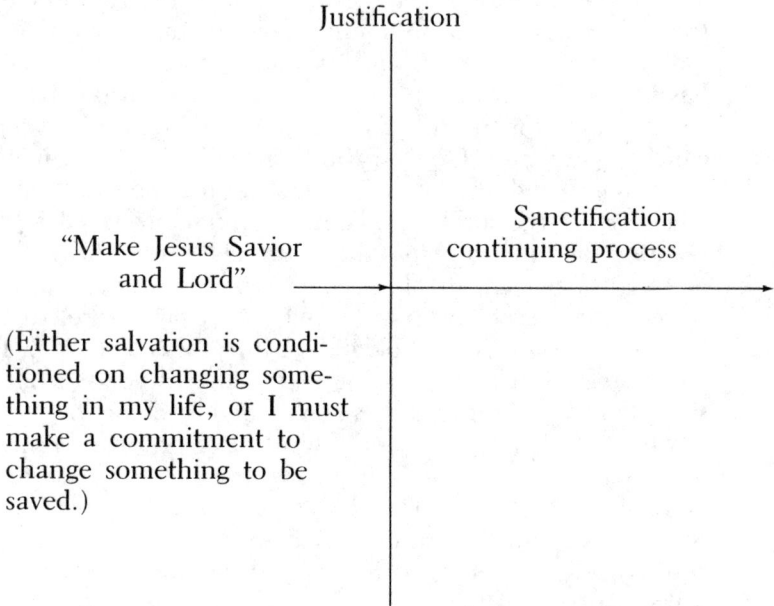

Justification

"Make Jesus Savior
and Lord"

Sanctification
continuing process

(Either salvation is conditioned on changing something in my life, or I must make a commitment to change something to be saved.)

Problem: a confusion of justification and sanctification (salvation partly by "works") right usually requires "going against the grain" in conscious acts of resolution. Sinning is easy; obedience is difficult—at least until we have developed new habits or patterns of life with the rewards of obedience quite consciously in view.

The tendency toward sin rather than toward obedience is especially evident in the life of the infant and child. Doing wrong, in my observation, never has to be taught, but obedience does. Children have a natural bent toward rebellion against parents; tell a child not to do something, and suddenly it becomes attractive. Even as an adult, Paul was honest enough to admit that he tended to do what he knew was wrong (See Romans 7).

Another misunderstanding is prevalent among some who teach that the spiritual life begins in earnest with a major, dedicatory event. This misunderstanding is found in the way they define "lordship." Lordship, they say, is a commitment distinct from the kind of faith required for one to be saved or justified. If such a commitment were required to be saved, it would amount to requiring a kind of human effort or "good works" for salvation. Saving faith, they argue, is simply trusting in Jesus as one's Savior; lordship is an entirely different issue.[4]

If lordship meant such things as giving up smoking and bad language, and letting Jesus become involved in all of one's decisions, then I would agree that such things are not the heart of the issue of salvation. Such things as these are involved in sanctification (Christian growth toward holiness), not justification.

But my concern is with the kind of faith that begins sanctification, and my fear is that an inadequate form of "faith" (a sort of mental assent) debilitates the visible

Sanctification

Fig. 2

VIEWS OF LORDSHIP
"Later Commitment" Theory

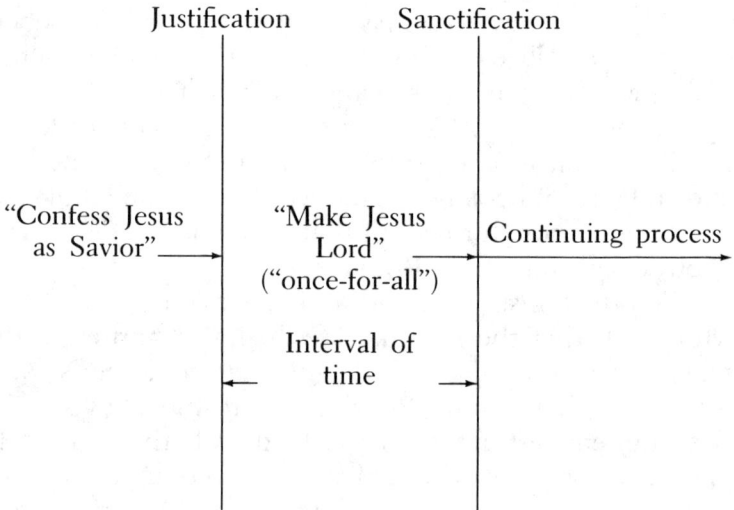

Justification   Sanctification

"Confess Jesus as Savior" ⟶ "Make Jesus Lord" ("once-for-all") ⟶ Continuing process

Interval of time

Virtues: Justification and sanctification are kept distinct; avoids salvation by "works."

Problems: Jesus as "Savior" is not clear. Does He save merely from hell or also from the power of sin from the beginning? It fails to do justice to Romans 10:9 and various discipleship passages in the Gospels. It may involve an inadequate concept of faith as mere intellectual assent.

church. People with this mental assent toward the savior-hood of Jesus do not want to make Jesus their Lord because they have already acquired all they want: mere forgiveness of sins without deliverance from sin. They live under the illusion that they have a ticket to heaven without the rigors of the Christian life.

Don't misunderstand me. On the one hand, I believe that justification is quite distinct from sanctification; but on the other hand, justification and sanctification are inseparable. One begins immediately where the other leaves off. Furthermore, I maintain that a very particular kind of faith is necessary for this to take place, a faith that affirms the sovereignty and authority of Jesus and that fully trusts Him to be the Savior.

It's my conviction that this is implicit in the decision to trust Christ as Savior from sin. Such a faith expects Jesus to deliver us from the power as well as the penalty of sin, and hence such faith expects Him to change our lives. It is also my conviction that this is implicit in repenting from sin. We do not acknowledge that we are sinners unless we want a change to take place in our rebellious attitude toward God. We then turn to Jesus to deliver us from our former state of alienation. This is what I mean by "lordship" (see the confession in Rom. 10:9).[5]

If we drive a wedge of time between salvation and lordship, we are in danger of giving the impression to some that lordship is an option that might be dispensed with, even if those who do so insist, as they do, that genuine salvation will inevitably lead to lordship in a matter of time.

Last of all, though giving up bad habits or specific sins is not necessarily a part of conversion, it is possible that such decisions could be concurrent with conversion,

Sanctification

Fig. 3

VIEWS OF LORDSHIP
"Historical View"

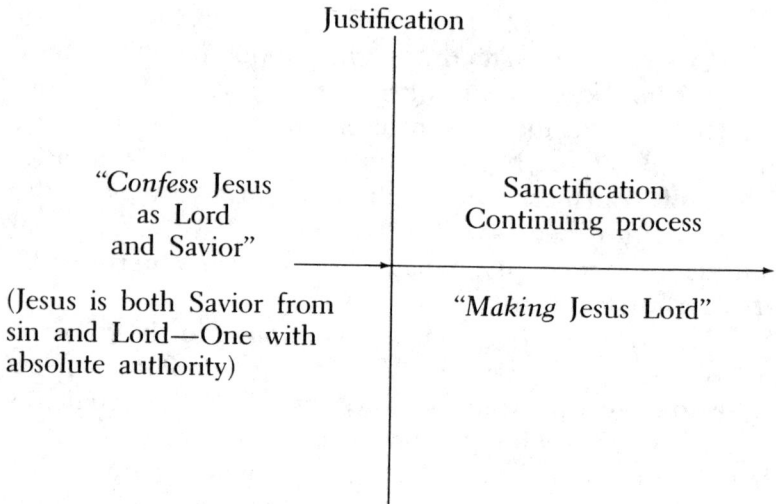

Justification

"*Confess* Jesus
as Lord
and Savior"

Sanctification
Continuing process

(Jesus is both Savior from
sin and Lord—One with
absolute authority)

"*Making* Jesus Lord"

Virtues: Justification and sanctification are kept distinct. "Works" are not involved in "confession," which is an act of faith. "Lord" in Romans 10:9 is understood in a natural sense. Retains concept of faith that is biblical (assent to truth as well as full trust).

depending on the background of the convert and the particular issue or situation that brought him or her to confess Christ as Savior. An alcoholic could stop drinking from the moment of conversion because that problem might be what the Lord used to bring that person to repentance and faith. Some habits and personal problems have a way of becoming spiritual issues after conversion because the implications of lordship gradually become clear as time progresses.

In summary: successful dealing with sin requires that we affirm (1) that we are living a new life (Rom. 6:1–11) and (2) that we have a new Master (Rom. 6:12–7:6). These affirmations of faith must penetrate our whole being and develop in us what is later called "a mind set on the Spirit" (Rom. 8:5–11), a totally new way of thinking about ourselves.

THE NEED FOR REPENTANCE

The next phase of the logic of Romans 6–8 is what we must "admit." In Romans 7 we find Paul's inner struggle that leads to this willingness to "admit." A transition takes place in Paul's thoughts from Romans 6 (what we must "affirm") to his struggle in chapter 7.

To illustrate the believer's freedom from the condemnation of the law and the need to affirm a new allegiance to righteousness, Paul compares the believer to a woman whose husband has died. The law binds her to that one man as long as he lives, but if he dies, she is free to marry another. Likewise, through identification with death in Christ, believers are delivered from the sin-dominion of the broken law and are free to give allegiance to Christ.

But believers must acknowledge this sin-dominion.

They also must believe that their sin is wrong and must want to change. This process is called "repentance."

But this illustration leads to a possible misunderstanding about law (Rom. 7:7), in which a person might think of the law itself as sinful. Paul lays this misunderstanding to rest by showing how the law functions in a way that makes a person conscious of sin (Rom. 7:7–13).

If the sin is as unrelenting as I believe it is, we will not automatically "affirm" what we should, nor will we "allow" the Holy Spirit to control us. Our tendency to sin leads us toward self-sufficiency or complacency, so that we need a new awareness of our inclination toward sin.

Let me explain it this way. Frequently a baseball player, though a good hitter or pitcher, enters into a period called a "slump." He goes out on the diamond thinking he will perform as well as he did the day before. Before long he realizes, through striking out or an inability to place his pitches in the strike zone, that he just doesn't have the "right stuff." What's so frustrating is that he can't figure out why he is playing so poorly. What does he need? He needs a batting or pitching coach to analyze his technique. A good coach is able to point out performance flaws and recommend what the player must do to correct them or compensate for them. This is the way God's law functions; like a good coach, God's law tells us where our behavior is wrong and where it needs to be changed. Moreover, it even lets us know, in spite of our blindness, that something is wrong.

This is repentance and personal revival. We all tend to decline over a period of time from even the most profound spiritual experiences. We fall back into subtle patterns of indifference and this makes us more susceptible to the more obvious forms of sin. We probably need to repent of something daily, whereas the need for revival, an extensive form of repentance, occurs periodically. We don't like to admit this because it's painful, too much like what Paul describes in Romans 7.

For us to carry through with our "affirmations" and allow the Holy Spirit to work effectively in us, we must consciously face up to the fact that if we don't repent, we inevitably will fail. God allows us to fail to teach us this. Of course this does not justify our sin.

Repentance is necessary for spiritual progress because of the nature of sin within us. We repent to get saved, and we repent to progress in salvation. This may be the very reason some professing Christians have never evidenced any change in their lives since they were "converted." They gave a mental assent to some facts about Jesus dying to pay for everyone's sin, thought it sounded good, and imagined or were told that they were "born again." But they had no intention of changing their lives, no recognition that anything was wrong with them.

I don't mean that we can reform ourselves. I'm talking about that despair of people who are lost, despair that causes them to turn to Jesus to deliver them from what they come to realize is a hopeless rebellion against God.

If I fell from a ship and began to drown, I would realize that I needed a life preserver to be saved. All the swimming I might try to do would not help me, and I would realize it. But if a life preserver were tossed to me, I would have to be willing to grasp it in faith that I could be retrieved and saved. I would want a "change" from being wet unto drowning to being dry unto saving.

But what does it mean to repent at the time of conversion? I am convinced that some forms of evangelism are carelessly or deliberately ignoring repentance as part of the gospel. Sometimes the problem is in understanding just what repentance is, and at other times the problem is in a reluctance to discuss a subject that may alienate the audience. One Evangelical theologian defines repentance as changing one's mind about Jesus Christ, a virtual synonym for faith.[6] While "changing one's mind" is indeed the root meaning of the Greek word for repentance, even a casual look at any concordance will show that it usually means a change of mind about sin.

Repentance is a change of attitude about our rebellious unbelief toward God.[7] This is why Jesus said that the Holy Spirit would convict the world of sin because they did not believe in Him (John 16:7–9). The epitome of sin is unbelief, not necessarily merely *dis*belief upon hearing the gospel, but the general state of mankind in its rebellion and ignorance of the true God. Repenting is simply admitting that we are sinners. Every gospel message in the Book of Acts requires repentance as part of the response that truly appropriates salvation.[8] In fact, even the words "believe" or "faith" do not always occur, but "repent" almost always does. Most standard works on theology view repentance as an aspect of conversion.[9] The other aspect is faith. Repentance is "negative"—what we turn away from by way of our attitude or will, and faith is "positive"—what we turn toward as the remedy of our sinful condition. Acts 20:21 brings out this relationship: ". . . solemnly testifying to both Jews and Greeks of repentance toward God and faith in our Lord Jesus Christ." That sometimes "believe" occurs without "repent" (Acts 16:31) and at other times "repent" appears without "believe" is probably because they are aspects of conversion and one implies the other, like the two sides of one coin. You can't have one without the other. Theologians may debate which comes first, but the important fact is that they are inseparable.

Repentance is vital to getting saved because repentance triggers a turning point in a person's life, so that his or her life changes as God does the changing. It's saying to God, "I know I need to change, and I know I can't change myself. Lord, will you change me?" Repentance prevents what some call "easy believism," an expression I do not particularly like. I prefer the expression "mental assent"; the word "believe" ought to be reserved for true saving faith. James 2:14–26, which challenges people to prove their faith by obedience to God, seems to be warning against mere mental assent. Demons "believe" in God, but they are not saved. I know of some people who say that they believe in Jesus Christ, but they show no evidence of it. I once quipped to a friend about one such person: "His faith isn't even as good as the faith of the demons—at least they tremble!"

Repentance still occupies a vital place in the lives of believers. They must continue to admit their sinful inclinations as part of being sanctified. They turn from sin to the One who can bring about change. The anatomy of this experience is provided in Romans 7.

PAUL VERSUS THE LAW

The apostle Paul seems to be reminiscing in Romans 7:7–13:

What shall we say then? Is the Law sin? May it never be! On the contrary, I would not have come to know sin except through the Law; for I would have not known about coveting if the Law had not said, "You shall not covet." But sin, taking opportunity through the commandment, produced in me coveting of every kind; for apart from the Law sin is dead. And I was once alive apart from the Law; but

> when the commandment came, sin became alive, and I died; and this commandment, which was to result in life, proved to result in death for me; for sin, taking opportunity through the commandment, deceived me, and through it killed me. So then, the Law is holy, and the commandment is holy and righteous and good. Therefore did that which is good become a cause of death for me? May it never be! Rather it was sin, in order that it might be shown to be sin by effecting my death through that which is good, that through the commandment sin might become utterly sinful.

Commentators offer several perspectives on this unusual passage, but I take the view that Paul is reflecting on his experience before his conversion, perhaps during his boyhood days.[10] Notice the verbs in the verses that follow the change to the present tense, while the verses quoted above are in the past tense. Paul uses the present tense to speak as Paul the Christian.

What value does the above passage have to us who are also now Christians? It tells us the way our sinful tendencies respond to God's law.

Observe several things. First, we come to "know" sin through the law (Rom. 7:7). This doesn't mean that we do not commit sin apart from the law (which Paul denies in Romans 5:13), but that we do not come to know sin for what it really is, an offense against God. Exposing ourselves daily to the Scripture is immensely important because it can bring us to repentance.

Next, notice how enlightening it is to see our sinful disposition's reaction to the law. According to Romans 7:8, the desire to sin is actually *aroused* by the commandment. Whatever is forbidden becomes attractive, but this means more than that. It is possible that Paul had in the back of his mind Adam's first sin in the Garden of Eden, especially when he uses the word "deceived." That first sin is a "model" for all other sin. The Serpent asked Eve, "'Indeed, has God said, "You shall not eat from any tree of the garden"?'" (Gen. 3:1), twisting the prohibition so that it sounded as if God was withholding something good rather than forbidding something bad. We react against this by rebelling and disobeying.

I don't mean that the more we read the Bible, the more we want to sin—perish the thought!—but that once the prohibition is placed in our minds, it at first begins a hankering to go ahead and do what the commandment forbids. Sin (or Satan) takes the commandment of God and exploits it by producing sin where there might be no sin. It becomes "alive." This again, seems to be a reference to Adam's being alive before his sin, and so in a very limited sense Paul was "alive"—unaware of the nature of sin—before the commandment came along.

Here there is an analogy, in a rough way at least, to our experience as believers. Through our exposure to the Scripture, we have developed an unconscious awareness of right and wrong. That which is wrong suddenly enters our consciousness in various ways; for example, a lurid advertisement in a magazine. There we are, minding our own business and in no conflict with God, when along comes this temptation. Desire for disobedience is aroused within, and if we don't check it, our desire will result in sin (James 1:14–15 expresses the same idea). Surely what I have just described is nothing we are not already aware of. What is novel is that the object of temptation is closely connected with God's prohibiting commandment. But watch out! It is sin, not God's law, that is the real culprit (Rom. 7:11–12).

Note one final idea in Romans 7:7–13. The law, or

Scripture, defines just what sin is. Earlier, in Romans 3:20, this was mentioned in passing: ". . . through the Law comes the knowledge of sin." Romans 7:13 takes this a step further. When sin takes advantage of "that which is good" (the law) to stir up sin in me, it betrays its true nature in the process. Death is the result. For believers, any one of many destructive results of sin could be involved, including death, if God did not graciously intervene in some kind of discipline (James 1:15; Heb. 2:4–13). Finally, after all of sin's promises have gone sour, we see the utter sinfulness of sin as a way that wrecks God's way of fulfillment.

WHAT WE MUST ADMIT

Now we come to Romans 7:14–24, one of the most difficult passages in the Bible. I am convinced that the present tense implies that Paul is looking at himself as a regenerated believer in contrast to his pre-regenerate days as a would-be lawkeeper (Rom. 7:7–13). Many Christians are reluctant to admit this, and understandably so. It comes as a shock for us to read what Paul says about himself in such a candid way because we have a tendency to romanticize historical figures, especially the great ones. Besides, the fourteenth verse seems to support the view that he is speaking as an unregenerate person when he says, "but I am of flesh, sold into bondage to sin."

But on the other hand, we find more or greater problems if we take what Paul says here as the words of an unregenerate person. For example, wouldn't it contradict the first three chapters of Romans to put the words, "I agree with the Law, confessing that it is good" (Rom. 7:16) or "I practice the very evil that I do not wish" (Rom. 7:19) or "the one who wishes to do good" (Rom. 7:21), or "I joyfully concur with the law of God in the inner man" (Rom. 7:22) into the mouth of a person who, apart from regeneration, suppresses the truth or always rebels against God, even if he were a religious Jew?

Our difficulty is in the stark contrast that exists between Romans 8 and Romans 7 here. We see no victory whatsoever in Romans 7, and we see nothing but victory in Romans 8. It is tempting, to make sense out of them, to place Paul's regeneration in Romans 7:25, as many in the past have done.

But if we do this, we will lose a great insight about ourselves: we vacillate between the experiences described in Romans 7 and Romans 8. They are not sequential in terms of an unregenerate then a regenerate. Instead, they are *aspects* of our Christian experience of regeneration. Why are they separated then? To emphasize the contrast between them. In Galatians 5:16–17 they are integrated to show their relationship: "For the flesh sets its desire against the Spirit, and the Spirit against the flesh; for these are in opposition to one another, so that you may not do the things that you please." Romans 7 depicts the flesh, while Romans 8 depicts the Spirit. Romans depicts no battle between the flesh and the Spirit, only the oppression of sin. Galatians suggests that the Spirit brings about a struggle between the flesh and the Spirit.

Romans 7 shows the utter hopelessness of action apart from the help of the Holy Spirit. In Galatians 5:16–17 it is clear that the only answer to fulfilling the desire of the flesh (our sinful disposition) is "walking in the Spirit." Therefore, in a manner similar to the decline of the Gentile, pagan world in Romans 1, there is an inevitable direction things will go if we allow them to do so.

One thing is clear in Romans 7:14–24. The sin

inclination or flesh is persistent and tends to dominate if we fail to check it. This explains the striking and alarming language in Romans 7:14: ". . . I am of flesh, sold into bondage to sin."[11] At first this does not seem possible for a regenerate person. Paul, however, is viewing himself from the narrow perspective of the inclination he has without the influence of the Holy Spirit.

Paul affirms several times (verses 15–17 and 19–23) that he really wants to do what is good. This is the desire of a regenerate person, one who is "partaker of the divine nature" (2 Peter 1:4). But this divine nature merely has the desire to do good. It lacks the ability. This is the essence of Romans 7:14–24. Being born again does not guarantee holiness apart from God's work through the Holy Spirit. The Holy Spirit is like a catalyst between this divine nature of which we partake and the righteousness that we are destined to do. Christian living is inevitable, in spite of our failures, as God energizes our wills and efforts. But it is never automatic. If this discourages you, it ought not to. You are now ready to say, "Wretched man that I am!" (Rom. 7:24). This is the thing that needs to be admitted. It is a healthy admission because it opens the door for Jesus Christ to set you free (Rom. 7:24) to be helped in the manner described in Romans 8.

WHAT WE MUST ALLOW

We all want to be in control of our lives. In the sense of accepting responsibility and making decisions without pressure from others, this is all right. But self-rule in opposition to God-rule is the very essence of sin. Adam committed this kind of sin.

As believers, we may be resistant to God's rule in our

lives partly because we misunderstand Jesus' lordship. The "yoke" of Jesus Christ is not all that oppressive, for Jesus Himself said, "Come to Me, all who are weary and heavy laden, and I will give you rest. Take My yoke upon you, and learn from Me, for I am gentle and humble in heart . . . for My yoke is easy, and My load is light" (Matt. 11:28–30). We are misled into thinking that the rule of Jesus Christ through the Holy Spirit is a constant compulsion to do everything we dislike, a life of despicable sacrifice. While it is quite true that self-denial is a part of dealing with our selfish tendencies, doing what pleases God becomes a delight once we have broken through our resistance.

This brings us to the crucial aspect of dealing with the power of sin. The Holy Spirit is within us, whether or not we are conscious of it (1 Cor. 6:19), for the purpose of dealing with sin, but we must allow Him to do His work. "It is God who is at work in you, both to will and to work for His good pleasure" (Phil. 2:13). This verse, along with the twelfth verse ("work out your salvation with fear and trembling"), contains the mystery of human responsibility to allow God to do something as well as the certainty that God will make us willing to allow Him to do it.

We are not likely to submit to God's work in our lives unless we are convinced that we have no decent alternative. Perhaps the shock value of knowing we will fail and mess up our lives is a necessary incentive to allow God to have His way, and apparently most of us need an occasional reminder.

First, Romans 8:1–11 explains the dynamics of the Spirit's control in our lives, resulting in obedience to God. Next, Romans 8:12–27 shows how the Spirit helps us toward this obedience.

Sanctification

Simply and profoundly, the words "There is therefore now no condemnation to those who are in Christ Jesus" (Rom. 8:1) sum up everything that has been said about our condemnation, justification, and lingering inward sin. What this means is that there is no legal barrier to God's working in us or in our being obedient to God. We are set free from sin's dominion by the "law" (or principle) of the "Spirit of life." Something starts to happen, which never happened during times when the law of Moses was in effect in Israel: the Holy Spirit dynamically works to accomplish more than the mere external pressure of the law ever accomplished. The law was weak "through the flesh" (human weakness here), but now the Holy Spirit is present to work within us and deal effectively with the sin tendency within us as well as to prod us in various ways to obedience. The prophet Jeremiah described it centuries ago as a new covenant that would write God's law on our hearts rather than on stone (Jer. 31:33).

Where do we fit in? We allow the Holy Spirit to do this by "walking" according to the Spirit. "Walking" is a metaphor for living. It's a good one because it suggests something that is continuous and that requires conscious dependence on our part. This dependence arises, as we have seen, out of our sense of need.

The same metaphor occurs in Galatians 5:16–17. Paul says that if we walk by the Spirit, we will not carry out "the desire of the flesh," probably a very broad category for any sort of disobedience to God, not merely sexual immorality or the like.

The picture of a person walking illustrates what the writer may even have implied. When we walk (according to my theory, at least), we actually fall forward. But we catch ourselves in this "fall" by stretching forth a leg and placing our weight on it. This dependence upon our legs in a movement we call walking is so unconscious that we long ago ceased to think much about it. But I imagine infants learning to walk for the first time are quite aware of what they are depending upon. People who have lost the use of their legs and must learn to walk all over again would probably know what I am talking about.

This illustration leaves us with two applications. First, "walking in the Spirit" is depending on the Holy Spirit to work through us. This doesn't mean that we become robots, but it means that we know we will fail if He doesn't energize whatever we do as we accept the responsibility to do it. I doubt that we necessarily feel anything happening; most of the time in my own experience, I look back upon the experience and recall a difference, and I look at the present and notice the good effect of what I did.

Second, the comparison between the infant and adult walking suggests that we could come to the point of habitually turning to the Spirit, and I hope we do. But our conscious dependence will always be a vital factor in walking in the Spirit.

Another expression in this passage is important. The Holy Spirit is in us to give us a "mind set upon" Him and the things of God (Rom. 8:6). This "mind" affects our desire or allegiance. It means that we are on God's side in the struggle against evil. In Galatians 5:16–17 it means that we have an inclination toward what the Spirit wants for us. Strangely, however, sin wins out over obedience if the Spirit is ignored, as we learned in Romans 7. Sin evidently has the ability to blind us temporarily to this desire for obedience in order for this phenomenon to take place.

In spite of the tendency of our good desires to succumb to the law of sin and death (Rom. 8:2), the Holy

Spirit is present to correct the tendency and bring us around to obedience in several ways (discussed in the next section). This happens to such an extent that our lives can actually be characterized as a whole as a "mind set on the Spirit"—a life of obedience. Romans 8:3–11 tells us there is no room for anything else. We can follow only two tracks, the "mind set on the flesh" or the "mind set on the Spirit." One leads to death, the other leads to life. Thus we must have before us here the contrasting lives of unregenerate people versus regenerate.

Paul says further that the Holy Spirit will make it possible to meet the "requirement of the Law" (Rom. 8:4). Romans 3:31 says that we "establish" the law through justification by faith. Faith does not circumvent the law. Through faith we are justified, and the barrier of condemnation is removed so that we can start becoming righteous.

The paradox will always remain: even though it sounds as if we are guaranteed a holy life as the result of the Spirit's work, we must allow the Spirit to do everything that He does. The provision mentioned in Romans 8:3–4 has been made "that the requirement of the Law might be fulfilled in us, who do not walk according to the flesh, but according to the Spirit." A truly regenerated, justified person will not "practice" sin (1 John 3:9). That person's course of life will be toward obedience and holiness. The regenerated person will commit sin, but sin will not dominate for any length of time. If it does, the person may well question the reality of his or her conversion.

Chapter Three

Implementing
the Solution:

The Great Promoter

The Quiet, Powerful Spirit
The Arrival of the Spirit
The Spirit Convicts
The Spirit Intercedes
The Spirit Teaches
The Spirit Helps Us Interpret
The Spirit Enables
Natural and Spiritual

THE QUIET, POWERFUL SPIRIT

The inner activity of the Holy Spirit is beyond the forefront of our consciousness. Some people dispute this because they have confused a purely psychological experience for the Holy Spirit.

It is easy to take this great activity within us for granted. Since our senses don't pick up the activity itself, but only some of its results, we are aware of its reality mainly by looking back on our experiences and noting the changes that have taken place, such as the "fruit of the Spirit" in our behavior and motivation. This is why I describe the inner work of the Holy Spirit as quiet and powerful.

This quiet, unobtrusive moving of the Holy Spirit made it necessary once for the apostle Paul to remind the Corinthians, "Do you not know that your body is a temple of the Holy Spirit who is in you?" (1 Cor. 6:19a). God can be within us, and we may have to be reminded of it! In the case of the Corinthians, such a condition resulted from their unholy preoccupations, but we also simply can take Him for granted.

How can we recognize the work of the Holy Spirit? Scripture describes several of the Holy Spirit's ministries, which have the ultimate purpose of promoting our spiritual life. I have deliberately chosen the word "promote," because the Holy Spirit never forces His work upon us. Instead, He prods us, gently pushes us, begs us, and exhorts us until we relent. Because we are "new creations" with a regenerated will, we *will* relent because we want to relent. Sometimes we resist vigorously, as if our true desire has been submerged beneath a sea of conflicting desires.

The Holy Spirit indwells each of us believers in Jesus Christ, and He exerts His influences from within our bodies, a most intimate resident. He makes the difference, the big difference, in the battle for obedience to God.

I am impressed by the difference between our ability to live godly lives and the ability of the Old Testament believers. The requirements for behavior definitely are higher in the New Testament than in the Old, in terms of character traits, at least. Paul suggests that we have a distinct advantage because we have the benefits of the Holy Spirit's new activities. "For what the Law could not do, weak as it was through the flesh, God did: sending His own Son in the likeness of sinful flesh and as an offering for sin, He condemned sin in the flesh, in order that the requirement of the Law might be fulfilled in us who do not walk according to the flesh, but according to the Spirit" (Rom. 8:3–4).

Old Testament believers appear to have experienced the Holy Spirit only selectively and periodically. We, on the other hand, have resources for spiritual living they did not have. The following chapters will describe them.

THE ARRIVAL OF THE SPIRIT

How and when did the Holy Spirit first become a resident? First Corinthians 12:13 links the arrival of the Holy Spirit with what it calls the "baptism" of the Spirit: "For by one Spirit we were all baptized into one body, whether Jews or Greeks, whether slaves or free, and *we were all made to drink of one Spirit*" (italics added). The metaphors seem to say that at the same time we are spiritually joined to other believers in common bond, we internally received the Holy Spirit. "Baptize" has the root meaning of dipping or submerging and thus carries with it the idea of incorporation and identification. This is similar to the idea expressed in Romans 6 that the believer is incorporated into the benefits of Jesus' death and resurrection. The past tense points to some event in the past when this happened for all believers.

Acts 2:38 confirms the idea that we receive the Holy Spirit at the time we repent—conversion, that is: "Repent, and let each of you be baptized in the name of Jesus Christ for the forgiveness of your sins; and you shall receive the gift of the Holy Spirit." John 3 teaches us that being born again happens by the Holy Spirit, and this implies that we receive Him at that time, which is, of course, our conversion.

Once the Holy Spirit enters our bodies, a unique relationship begins. Think how strange and remarkable this event, which first occurred at Pentecost, must have been to those first Christians. Jesus had tried to prepare them for it when He promised His coming: "And I will ask the Father, and He will give you another Helper, that He may be with you forever; that is the Spirit of truth, whom the world cannot receive, because it does not behold Him or know Him, but you know Him because He abides with you, and will be in you" (John 14:16–17).

Note two important words in this verse: "forever" and the preposition "in," which is contrasted with the preposition "with." The word "forever" stresses permanence, and "in" describes a new, intimate relationship. It's not as if the word "in" had never been used before of the Holy Spirit (see, for example, Genesis 41:38), but Jesus' point is that something new and different would take place.

The sum of it is this: The Holy Spirit has been "with" God's people to help them accomplish mighty works, like Jesus' earlier ministry, described in Matthew 10. But until Pentecost, the Spirit was not indwelling permanently. He had departed from Samson (Judg. 15:14; 16:20) and from King Saul (1 Sam. 10:10; 18:12), and David had prayed that the Holy Spirit might not be taken from him (Ps. 51:11).

The difference is like the difference between someone coming to *visit* and someone coming to *live*. Both are going to be *in* my house, but one will be gone after the visit is complete, while the other is coming to stay. The Spirit now indwells the believer to stay, permanently.

Consider the evidence of this permanence in the New Testament. According to Ephesians 1:13 and 4:30, the believer is "sealed" by the Holy Spirit until "the day of redemption." The implication is that this seal won't be broken.

So the believers baptized in the Holy Spirit at Pentecost had received the Holy Spirit in a new way. Besides being with them forever, the Holy Spirit began to do some new things that He had never done before. They all result in a more comprehensive influence on our minds and wills. For one thing, as we noted earlier, God's law is "written on the heart" (Jer. 31:33–34).

The Holy Spirit often makes a difference from the earliest moments or days of a new believer's life. I remember the remarkable change in the attitude of a Jewish atheist. Before his conversion, he found problems and inconsistencies everywhere in the Bible, even where common sense would have told him they didn't exist. But after he finally acknowledged his attitude of rebellion and confessed Christ, he—almost overnight—began to read the Bible as a message from God.

This indwelling Spirit brings about a control of our lives that is expressed by such striking language as "walking by the Spirit," "led by the Spirit," and "filled with the Spirit." These all appear in the form of commands, indicating that we have a part in bringing them about.

THE SPIRIT CONVICTS

When Jesus promised the Comforter or Holy Spirit, He said that the Spirit would convict the world of sin, righteousness, and judgment (John 16:7–11). Since this Comforter is "another" comforter (John 14:16), He is actually taking over some of Jesus' works. The words "because they do not believe in Me" (John 16:9) clarify what conviction of sin means: that all mankind is in a state of separation or alienation from God and the only remedy is to believe in Jesus Christ (see John 20:31).

Even though this convicting work of the Holy Spirit affects the world as a whole, according to Jesus' language, it surely doesn't stop when we become Christians; we still need to be convicted of sin. Logic tells us that such things as the changing of our character require conviction of sin.

How does the Spirit convict us of sin? One way is by bringing the Word of God to our consciousness, identifying sin, and exposing it for what it really is, "utterly sinful" (Rom. 7:13). The Spirit gives us a deep-seated desire to please God, and we eventually respond with remorse like David's: "For I know my transgressions, and my sin is ever before me. Against Thee, Thee only, I have sinned, and done what is evil in Thy sight, so that Thou art justified when Thou dost speak, and blameless when Thou dost judge" (Ps. 51:3–4).

Note that David says, "my sin is ever before me." The

Spirit does convict. I have been struck often by the psychological power of communist indoctrination. From photographs of scenes in China and the Soviet Union, I have been impressed that people in those countries are under the spell of immense portraits of Mao and Lenin as well as challenging slogans on billboards everywhere they go. Even in their passing thoughts, communist doctrine enters their minds over and over again. Likewise, the Holy Spirit confronts us with biblical truth on the "billboards" of our minds to convict us of sin. I once did housecleaning for a fairly wealthy woman. As I recall, I did my best work in the living room, where her portrait hung!

Recognizing our sin is not the end of the matter, however. We can expect a struggle. Paul is probably thinking about the convicting power of the Spirit when he describes how the Spirit "strongly desires" (the literal meaning of "sets its desire") against the flesh. The picture is of two opposing desires, one of the flesh and the other of the Spirit, evil as opposed to good. Each vies for our decision in a spiritual or moral situation. At first you might think that once these issues are so clear, our basic disposition to go with God would automatically win out. Where is the struggle in such a situation?

The answer is twofold. First, merely recognizing that something is sin does not mean that we wholeheartedly embrace what is right. We resist the dictates of our consciences. We rationalize what we inwardly, at the "gut level," know is wrong. This could occupy us for a while, perhaps days, weeks, even months. When we set our hearts on some enterprise, we don't like to be denied. Sometimes we go ahead and commit sin and eventually become convinced at the level of our wills that we must stop it. But the Spirit persists within us to throw to us the truth of God's Word until our resistance is broken down.

Second, we often fail to perceive the sinfulness of an issue because of barriers that we have erected over a period of time. The Holy Spirit must demolish these, too. These barriers are usually attitudes that we have nourished over a time and have become unconscious of. For example, a prejudice may constitute one of these barriers. Let's say I have developed a bad feeling toward a neighbor to the extent that I consider him spiritually hopeless. I avoid sharing my faith with him or refuse to encourage him in his faith. Nobody is to be thought of as hopeless. Paul may have had such an attitude toward John Mark, who had deserted him on the first missionary journey (Acts 15:37–39), so that Paul was unwilling to give Mark another chance.

The Spirit not only works within us, but He also uses circumstances and other people. These means shock us into reality either because they teach us that we cannot control a situation or because they let us know that someone else knows about our sin. Similarly, the Spirit uses preaching, teaching, and personal relationships with our fellow believers. I suppose the ideal is the inner working of God's Word that has become part of our deep-seated convictions. This Scripture that we have "treasured" within us, can either prevent or abort sin before it gets to the stage of action (Ps. 119:11).

If you get convicted of sin the way David did in Psalm 51, you have the surest evidence of your redemption and regeneration. You also sense that you have hurt the God whom you love. Unbelievers who are sorry for their sin are not sorry because they have hurt God, but because their sin may have tarnished their image or their sin may have caused them embarrassment. But like David, the true believer realizes, "Against Thee, Thee only, have I sinned, and done what is evil in Thy sight, so that Thou art justified when Thou dost speak, and blameless when Thou dost judge" (Ps. 51:4).

THE SPIRIT INTERCEDES

Prayer is hard work for a number of reasons, but we have help. The Spirit "intercedes" in our prayer: ". . . the Spirit also helps our weakness; for we do not know how to pray as we should, but the Spirit Himself intercedes for us with groanings too deep for words; and He who searches the hearts knows what the mind of the Spirit is, because He intercedes for the saints according to the will of God" (Rom. 8:26–27).

"Our weakness" probably means our human limitations in general, specified here as not knowing how to pray as we should. When it comes to making a decision, "our weakness" is not knowing the best course of action in some situation. Even after we have searched the Scripture for wisdom, we may face several options that appear to be equally wise. That's when we need help.

The Spirit's "groanings" are deep desires for what is best for us, a meaning that is in accord with the other two "groanings" in the previous context (Rom. 8:22–23). They are intercessory; that is, they come in at the point where our prayers are otherwise ineffective because we don't know what is best. I like to think of them as connecting links between our ineffective prayers and God's wisdom. The Spirit's intercessory groanings bridge the gap, making our prayers effective. If this interpretation is correct, we might pray one thing while the Holy Spirit prays another, in some instances. But, beautifully, this is not conflict; it is harmony! Let's look at it in terms of another word: our otherwise inadequate but fervent prayer is "translated" into prayer according to God.

This reminds me of a sermon I once preached in a Chinese church, using an interpreter. I was trying to make a point and spoke for quite a while before stopping to let the translator take over. Amazingly, he took much less time to put what I had said into the foreign dialect. Later, I asked him how he did it. His reply was, "Some of the things you said were virtually impossible to translate so that the people could understand, but I knew what you were really trying to say and merely put it in a different way!" If our hearts are right, our inaccurate prayers are simply put a different way so God can answer them according to His wisdom.

This is possible because the Holy Spirit, the third member of the triune Godhead, indwells us and intimately knows us and our situation. Since each member of the Godhead is in complete harmony and unity, this information is communicated One to the Other. This is what is meant by the words, "He who searches the hearts knows what the mind of the Spirit is " (Rom. 8:27a). God the Father is the Searcher via the Holy Spirit. What a fascinating insight to the mechanics of God's omnipresence!

None of this should lead us to think that prayer can be careless or irrational. This divine operation works only when our inadequacies are due to our human limitations. Elsewhere in the Bible prayer is rational, specific, and knowledgeable.

THE SPIRIT TEACHES

The Holy Spirit teaches as no one else can; His work in communicating truth is in a class by itself. He helps us interpret the Bible, grasp its truth (known as "illumination"), and perceive the spiritual significance of all that the Bible contains, things that are beneath the surface or less obvious.

Jesus Himself, the Master Teacher, called the Holy Spirit a teacher because He would guide the apostles into all the truth (John 16:13–14). Another important passage, 1 John 2:20, 27, probably refers to the Holy Spirit: "But you have an anointing from the Holy One, and you all know. . . . And as for you, the anointing which you received from Him abides in you, and you have no need for any one to teach you; but as His anointing teaches you about all things, and is true and is not a lie, and just as it has taught you, you abide in Him."

Since the word "anointed" is used in Luke 4:18 of the Holy Spirit's anointing of Jesus to "preach the gospel to the poor" (see also Acts 10:38) and since 2 Corinthians 1:21–22 talks of our being anointed and given the Holy Spirit, I am convinced that John's reference to the "anointing" also means anointing by the Holy Spirit. The "Holy One" is Jesus, the One who anoints at Pentecost with the Holy Spirit, and John's point is that we are not enslaved to any teachers as the sole source of truth, like the early Gnostic teachers at Ephesus to whom John refers.

John is not telling us that all human teachers are unnecessary because he himself was a teacher by virtue of the fact that he was an apostle. Furthermore, teaching itself is a gift given to certain people who work closely with the pastors of the church (Eph. 4:11). The context of 1 John 2 implies that the false teachers at Ephesus were probably teaching new "truth" and adding to the teachings of the apostles. We do not need anyone to add teachings to the body of truth that is now complete, "the faith . . . once for all delivered to the saints" (Jude 3). The teachers of the church merely clarify this body of truth for the believers to equip them for service (Eph. 4:12).

Three subjects work together to produce learning of spiritual truth, which in turn gets translated into obedience to Christ: the Holy Spirit, the gifted teacher, and the student. Without this "triangle," learning can take place but not the learning of biblical truth. Such learning is distinctive because its goal is different from ordinary learning. Ordinary education seeks to impart knowledge and skills, but biblical instruction has as its goal "love from a pure heart and a good conscience and a sincere faith" (1 Tim. 1:5).

Let's take a closer look at this "triangle":

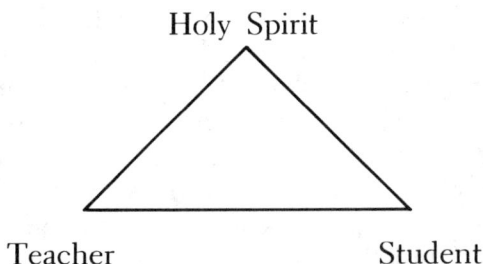

Holy Spirit

Teacher   Student

Starting with the Holy Spirit, two functions occur. First, the Holy Spirit helps the teacher creatively explain the meaning of Scripture and how it applies to the student's life. The teacher must be willing to let the Spirit do this and must be concerned only for the accuracy of the teaching, not embellishing it with fancy and extraneous ideas or "gimmicks." Second, the Holy Spirit helps the student understand the teacher's communication. The student must acknowledge the authority of Scripture and respect the office of the teacher. The student, too, must have a proper relationship with the Holy Spirit to be illumined and exhorted to obey the truth.

Take it from another approach. We read in 1 Corinthians 2:9–16 that the "natural" person (the unregenerate, who does not accept the things of the Spirit of God because they are foolishness to him or her) cannot participate in spiritual learning. On the other hand, the "spiritual" person (the regenerate person with the Holy Spirit) is able to "appraise" all things, evaluate the worth of things from the standpoint of God's wisdom (thus the implication of the context). The Holy Spirit allows us to perceive the things of God and thus to view the true importance and value of the whole world and everything that is in it. This is information wedded to God's wisdom.

The Holy Spirit also reveals to us things beyond our sensory perception (1 Cor. 2:9). This opens up the very thoughts of God (1 Cor. 2:11) and puts them into humanly understandable words (1 Cor. 2:13). Finally, as our "teacher," the Holy Spirit imparts to us the very "mind of Christ" (1 Cor. 2:16), the ability—with the use of Scripture, I believe—to think like Christ. One way this happens is through studying Jesus' thinking in the Gospel records and transferring His thinking to similar situations.

When Jesus called the Holy Spirit a teacher in John 14:26, His primary reference was to the future inspiration of the New Testament, but this verse also describes how the Holy Spirit works with our minds, making available what we have put into them through reading and memorization. Jesus told the disciples that the Holy Spirit would bring to their remembrance everything that He had taught them. Evidently the Spirit would activate their memories, helping them recall Jesus' words and works. We may not associate this sort of activity with teaching, but when it comes to God's revelation, the implementation of truth is a part of the total process.

Since the Holy Spirit is called "another Helper," corresponding to Jesus, it follows that the Holy Spirit must teach as Jesus did. At first this seems impossible because Jesus was bodily present with His disciples, and they could watch Him continually. But when you think about it, the church as a whole is involved in teaching, and through the teachers in the church, the Holy Spirit is doing what Jesus did.

Remember what that was. Jesus lived day after day with His students. They were able to watch Him in every conceivable circumstance and see how His teachings about life and God were carried out in practice; Jesus modeled the truth to His students. His ultimate goal was that they, like good students of any good teacher, would come to be like Him (Matt. 10:25). People can learn facts by merely listening to their teachers, but watching the truth in action provides the best possible incentive to practice the truth.

Most genuine teaching takes place outside the class-room. In this sense, we all are teachers, but to be good teachers we need the Holy Spirit to teach through us. Take the family, for example. Parents need to do a lot of teaching on the spot, and the Holy Spirit gives them awareness and wisdom to do this through moments of instruction at just the right occasion and through their general attitudes. For instance, if parents want their kids to be honest, the parents must be honest in all their dealings. Likewise, in the church we all are instruments of the Holy

Spirit's teaching. In formal groups, we should follow the techniques of Jesus, the Master Teacher, and then live what we teach.

In summary, the teaching function of the Holy Spirit goes beyond what is normally included in education on the ordinary level. Spiritual truth requires perception of a supernatural nature. The Holy Spirit removes the obstacles of deceit and rebellion within us, enlightens our minds, activates our memories, and shows us in the lives of others how to live godly lives.

THE SPIRIT HELPS US INTERPRET

In addition to teaching us, the Holy Spirit also helps us interpret God's Word. The Spirit "illuminates," helping us interpret the Bible in an honest, scientific way.

Biblical interpretation, also called hermeneutics, is a "science" because it requires us to use logical principles. Briefly stated, these logical principles are examining a passage's historical background, analyzing its context, defining the meaning of words in their cultural setting, comparing a passage with the rest of the Bible, and identifying the "genre" of the passage (what kind of literature it is).

You might wonder what place the Holy Spirit could have in such scholarly pursuits as these. I am convinced that the Spirit's work is not an easy shortcut that bypasses hard work. Biblical interpretation is usually tedious and demanding but immensely rewarding because it gets you to understand the very Word of God as it should be understood today. In other words, biblical interpretation tries to understand exactly what the biblical writer was saying to his or her generation, who understood it as clearly as we understand the daily newspaper. The Bible contains no hocus-pocus or hidden meanings, just plain, everyday language. That's the way the Bible was written. Religious charlatans like to make it mysterious and obscure.

What role does the Holy Spirit have in scientific biblical interpretation? Let's call it "intercessory." Two things prevent us from discovering the biblical author's meaning: one is our sinful unwillingness to face the truth that is obvious from the biblical text, and the other is our inability to perceive the significance of biblical truth, how it relates in a meaningful way to our lives.

Let's take the first of these. Through His work in conviction of sin, the Holy Spirit prods us to greater honesty as we apply the techniques of biblical interpretation. It takes expertise to use the various principles mentioned above. God has called some scholars to devote their lives to technical aspects of biblical studies, but godliness is a prerequisite in order for us to be absolutely objective. From the scholar pondering an exotic text from Ebla to the teacher preparing to do an exposition of the biblical text, each person must put aside prejudices and honestly look at Scripture. We must be willing to allow Scripture to expose our inner selves, even if we see things we do not like to see. This work of the Holy Spirit comes to bear upon the moments of decision when we interpret and apply God's Word.

The second obstacle that prevents us from getting at the biblical author's meaning or intention is our human limitation in grasping the spiritual significance of something. Sometimes we fail to see something that could warm our hearts, excite us, or challenge us to a personal response.

Sanctification

Take the simple historical narrative of Acts 16:6–10, which records some incidents during Paul's second missionary journey. Paul and his friends had passed through the Phrygian and Galatian region and were strangely prevented by the Holy Spirit from entering into Asia as they had intended. Turning north, they traveled toward Bithynia but were again stopped from entering that province. Eventually they wound up at Troas on the Aegean coast. Here Paul had a vision of a man pleading for him to come to Macedonia, westward across the Aegean. The next morning Paul told his companions about the vision, and they all concluded that it was God's will to go to Macedonia. These are the facts of the narrative, but is that all there is to it? No, I believe not. This passage can become important in providing insights for making decisions that are not morally clear-cut.

Let's look more closely and note some helpful items. Notice that sometimes God intervenes in decisions that seem to be wise choices but are contrary to His purpose. Also notice that while God gives insight, it is also proper and profitable to discuss some decisions with other believers. This is brought out in the word "they concluded," which literally means "they put it all together." In other words, the team carefully evaluated all the events, taking into account the vision and the Holy Spirit's intervention on two occasions, and they made a joint decision.

The truth and application I have just drawn from this historical situation starts with the hermeneutical principles but goes farther. I believe that the Holy Spirit helps us see such things, that such observation is more than ingenuity or logic. It is seeing the spiritual dimension of something. Be careful, for such interpretation must rest squarely on grammar and the meaning of words (exegesis). Nevertheless, the Holy Spirit activates our spiritual perception because such things are "spiritually perceived" (1 Cor. 2:14).

THE SPIRIT ENABLES

The spiritual life is a supernatural life. It begins supernaturally with the gracious intervention of God in drawing us to Jesus Christ, and since what begins in such a remarkable way must continue that way, it must be continually and supernaturally energized by God's grace. As Paul puts it, "Having begun by the Spirit, are you now being perfected by the flesh?" (Gal. 3:3). The answer is, of course, "No!"

We're ready to look at the expression "be filled with" the Spirit, an expression widely misunderstood. Two biblical writers use this expression to describe how the Holy Spirit graciously enables us to do what we could not do for ourselves. Grace is needed at conversion, and grace is needed during sanctification. Some scholars erroneously define "filled with" the Spirit as "baptism," which is the reception of the Holy Spirit at Pentecost. The best way to begin is to review some passages that use the word "filled" and see what they say about it.

> And they were all filled with the Holy Spirit and began to speak with other tongues, as the Spirit was giving them utterance (Acts 2:4).

> Then Peter, filled with the Holy Spirit, said to them. . . . Now as they observed the confidence of Peter and John, and understood that they were uneducated and untrained men, they were marveling, and began to recognize them as having been with Jesus (Acts 4:8, 13).

And when they had prayed, the place where they had gathered together was shaken, and they were all filled with the Holy Spirit, and began to speak the word of God with boldness (Acts 4:31).

. . . And they chose Stephen, a man full of faith and of the Holy Spirit, . . . yet they were unable to cope with the wisdom and the Spirit with which he was speaking (Acts 6:5, 10).

"Brother Saul, the Lord Jesus, who appeared to you on the road by which you were coming, has sent me so that you may regain your sight, and be filled with the Holy Spirit." . . . And immediately he began to proclaim in the synagogues, saying, "He is the Son of God" (Acts 9:17, 20).

And do not get drunk with wine, for that is dissipation, but be filled with the Spirit, speaking to one another in psalms and hymns and spiritual songs, singing and making melody with your heart to the Lord; always giving thanks for all things in the name of our Lord Jesus Christ to God, even the Father; and be subject to one another in the fear of Christ (Eph. 5:18–21).

The thing that stands out in these passages is the boldness and ability to proclaim the Word of God as a result of the filling of the Spirit. The phenomenon of speaking in tongues raises some questions, and Charismatic believers are opposed to many other believers on the issue of whether such a phenomenon exists today in its authentic New Testament form, but I am not concerned at this point with that matter. Both factions will agree with one thing: when the Holy Spirit "fills" us, the reticence that often accompanies our proclaiming the gospel to others is removed, and the gospel is boldly and clearly presented.

The passage from Ephesians (5:18–21) is the most

definitive. We need to realize first that the metaphor "fill" has nothing to do with greater quantity.[1] It pertains to *influence*, complete and comprehensive. When the Spirit fills, He effectively exerts control over us, enabling us to accomplish things beyond our ordinary abilities or inclinations. The comparison to drunkenness fits this well, for the quantity of wine is not the most important factor in being drunk—for different people are differently affected by varying amounts. Intoxication or influence is the important factor.

Observe something else. The verb "be filled" is a present imperative, which may imply an ongoing, life-characterizing filling. The filling of the Spirit is not some emotionally induced religious experience, a spiritual "high." It is a way of life.

The verses that follow (Eph. 5:19–21) teach this way of life. Verse 19 gives us a peek into an apostolic worship service where some form of antiphonal singing took place ("speaking to one another"). The singing was joyous and heartfelt, pure worship of the Lord. Jesus said that worship should be "in Spirit" (John 4:24). Verse 20 makes reference to continuous thanksgiving for *all* things, meaning both the good and the unpleasant. Finally, verse 21 concludes the string of related participles—"speaking," "singing," "making melody," and "giving thanks"—with "being subject" to one another (literal translation). This means putting the welfare of others ahead of our own as well as submitting to others, and it takes various kinds of forms depending who is doing it, as the verses that follow show. It is such a fundamental attitude toward one another that Paul is required to show how it works out in all the domestic relations we have.

For a wife, subjection is allowing the husband to

exercise his role of "head" and to do it "as to the Lord," which means her primary obedience is to Christ, although it might mean that she obeys her husband in the same way she would the Lord. For a husband, subjection means he loves his wife as unselfishly as Christ loves the Church. For children, it means obeying parents as if they were representatives of the Lord. The slaves were to submit to their masters as if they were pleasing Jesus Christ, and masters were to exercise their authority, remembering that they, too, had a Master in heaven.

Notice how the Lord Jesus Christ is the reason why each is subject to the other. Each has his or her own role and relationship and each submits as if submitting to the Lord.

The filling of the Spirit is living a life of unselfishness and service to others and the Lord. It's a way of making the most of one's time, of being wise, of guaranteeing that God's will gets done.

How is the filling of the Spirit achieved? It's fairly obvious that we must face sin squarely and honestly, making us conscious of our need for a working relationship with God. We must *affirm*, *admit*, and *allow*.

A further clue to how we can be filled with the Spirit is found in Galatians 5:16–17, which stresses the idea of dependence. The desires of the flesh are pitted against those of the Holy Spirit, so that we are not able to do what we "please," that which is good (Rom. 7:15–19). This dilemma is resolved by walking in the Spirit. In practical terms, what does that mean? It's saying to ourselves, "Lord, I am stymied. This desire to do evil is powerful and attractive, and I am morally weak. But I know if I give in to my evil desires, the outcome will be disappointment, heartache, and ultimately death. I really want to please

you as your child. I therefore resolve heartily to let the
Spirit take over. I determine to do what is right as He works
in me."

Let me illustrate it another way and in a more spiritual
and less moral situation. Let's say I have an opportunity to
present the gospel. Witnessing to strangers has always
frightened me, partly because I am shy and an introvert.
But that's no excuse. The flesh makes me inclined to keep
to myself and mind my own business, to avoid making a
fool out of myself. The Spirit prods me to say something,
to be friendly, to look for an opportunity to say something
about the Lord. Deep inside me I believe that I should
witness to people, that evangelism is one of the most
important of all occupations, that I am part of God's plan
for winning the lost to Christ. I can do one of two things. I
can ignore the quiet "voice" of the Holy Spirit or I can
obey it. I sense my inadequacy. I don't have anything in
common with this person. My mind tends to go blank, and
I forget to use Bible verses I have learned. But suddenly I
remember the consequences of not witnessing, my sense
of guilt, the loss of joy in failing to participate with God in
communicating the truth, the fear of being partly account-
able for a person's going into eternity without Christ. I
remember that the Spirit can bring things to my memory
and cause Christ to be seen in me, making the truth
powerful. I remember that the Spirit can work in this
person and open his or her heart to the truth. I brush aside
all my restraints and plunge into the conversation with a
sense of dependency on the Spirit.

What happened? I "walked" in the Spirit. Believing He
would help me, I did what I could the best way I knew
how. Later, whether or not I had been successful in
introducing this person to Christ, I determined to be better

prepared by thinking about the questions and problems people thrust at me. But I later realized that I would always need the Spirit to put it all together successfully.

When the Holy Spirit promotes within us such a life, we can expect a growing degree of consistent obedience. We'll have our relapses. Extended periods of indifference to sin should alarm us, so that we take inventory of our salvation. Though at first glance this last statement may appear to be a denial of the assurance of salvation that the Bible teaches is possible, it simply means that we should never take salvation for granted. We need evidence to assure us of our salvation just as a wife repeatedly needs her husband's assurance that he loves her.

Listen to Scripture: "Test yourselves to see if you are in the faith; examine yourselves! Or do you not recognize this about yourselves, that Jesus Christ is in you—unless indeed you fail the test?" (2 Cor. 13:5). "Therefore, brethren, be all the more diligent to make certain about His calling and choosing you; for as long as you practice these things, you will never stumble" (2 Pet. 1:10). We should be practicing: "faith . . . moral excellence . . . self-control . . . godliness . . . brotherly kindness . . . love" (2 Pet. 1:5–7).

Vital Christian living involves frequent repentance, a quality that made David a man "after God's heart." We must examine ourselves for a desire for God's Word, a sense for the need of prayer, and a concern for others. True, these things are frequently lacking, but does it concern us that they are? If it does, then we have a sign that the Holy Spirit is promoting obedience to God within us, a sign that we are genuinely "in the faith."

In the next chapter we will examine what spirituality is all about. As we do, we will overlap into some matters we have already discussed. One of the important questions in the present Evangelical church is: Can a genuine believer live forever as a "carnal" believer?

NATURAL AND SPIRITUAL

"Spiritual" is the Bible's way of putting into one word the essence of the spiritual life. But today it's an ambiguous term in our society and an abused term in the church. We need to define it before we use it further.

Outside of the Christian environment the term "spiritual" means a person who is not materialistic, whose values do not center on money. The "spiritual" person is a lover of cultural things such as good music, art, knowledge, and literature. Actually this use of "spiritual" is not entirely foreign to the biblical use, but it fails to identify the essence of biblical spirituality.

Unfortunately, the word "spiritual" is also connected with spiritism or things of the occult, the belief in the presence and activity of those who have died but remain active in this world in some way. This use of the term is totally foreign to the biblical idea.

The Bible uses the word *spiritual* in a number of ways. "Spiritual" may be defined as "pertaining to the Spirit" or "characterized by the Spirit" in its usage in 1 Corinthians 2:13–3:4. In other places, like 1 Corinthians 15:44 or Ephesians 1:3, it seems to be used in the sense of "related to the heavenly."[2]

First Corinthians 2:14–15 uses the word "spiritual" in contrast to the word "natural." Other expressions such as "babes in Christ," and "fleshly" ("carnal" KJV) are related to it in the same context (1 Cor. 3:1–3). But the fact that the "spiritual" person is able to "accept the things of the Spirit of God" and that all believers have received the Holy Spirit leads me to the conclusion that the world consists of just two kinds of persons, natural and spiritual, and the other expressions above are merely subdivisions within the category of spiritual.[3]

This point of view is in conflict with a widespread opinion that spirituality is a goal to be achieved, not a quality that every believer possesses. The statement that the spiritual person "appraises all things" (1 Cor. 2:15) has been interpreted to apply only to the mature believer who has the developed ability to perceive things much more intelligently and biblically than a fellow believer who has been recently converted. But an ability may be in an undeveloped state, something that will grow with exercise. A genuine new believer shows signs from the earliest moments of new life that he or she looks at things differently, even though this new perspective may not be readily apparent to the outsider. In the modern Evangelical church, this new perspective goes undetected because we fail to disciple new believers. Frequently new believers merely pick up the characteristics of other complacent Christians, and their new capacity to appraise all things goes undeveloped.

Appraisal is the process of putting God's evaluation on things, of getting a biblical perspective. It's looking at the whole world differently, "the old things passed away; . . . new things have come" (2 Cor. 5:17). This is true of all who are "in Christ," thus, it is true of even the newest believer.

Many new Christians can testify to the immediate, though often subtle, change of attitude when they first confess Christ as Savior. Repentance starts a revolution that eventually pervades a person's thinking. The person begins to grow through the infusion of the Holy Spirit. Spirituality comes from new birth, maturity by growth.

Maturity and spirituality are not exactly the same, though they are related. Spirituality corresponds to the characteristics we receive at birth, those things we inherit from our parents. We are partakers of the divine nature just as we are partakers of our parents' natures. These qualities can be seen in children in incomplete ways, and they develop and mature as children grow up. Spirituality is built into every believer. We are given qualities that make us appear different from who we were, qualities characteristic of God Himself. With growth they flower and become beautiful.

The Bible does not command us to be spiritual, but it does tell us to be mature or "perfect." The idea of "mature" is bound up in the biblical word often translated "perfect." When we read the word "perfect" in some of our English translations of the Bible, we often assume it means what we mean by it today. The word essentially means "to progress toward a goal" as can clearly be seen in Philippians 3:13–15: "Brethren, I do not regard myself as having laid hold of it yet [Paul refers to perfect knowledge of Christ and conformity to Him]; but one thing I do: forgetting what lies behind and reaching forward to what lies ahead, I press on toward the goal for the prize of the upward call of God in Christ Jesus. Let us therefore, *as many as are perfect* have this attitude" (italics added). The word "mature" is a better rendering, but even it fails to capture the dynamic nature of continual growing.

If it is true that all believers are spiritual, the implications are serious. It should arouse us to greater zeal to realize the potential that is truly ours. We have tended to reserve such a designation for an elite few in the body of

Christ, a few "supersaints" whom we believe have sufficiently and sacrificially attained to a quality of Christian living.

We can behave spiritually anytime we want to obey God, and steady growth toward consistency in spiritual behavior—maturing—is the norm and the inevitable direction we are all going.

Chapter Four

Clarifying

Basic Questions:

The Meaning of "Spirituality"

The Way We Used To Be
A Prevalent Misconception
Growing Without Pain
Growing in Trials
Growing Through Discipline
Growing Through
  Responsibility
Discipleship
Decision Making

THE WAY WE USED TO BE

Sometimes we act as if we are unbelievers. Sound shocking? Well, I mean that we behave like unbelievers, not that we suddenly stop believing in Christ. We sometimes act the way we used to act before we became believers.

Paul describes such people as "carnal" Christians (1 Cor. 3:1–4 KJV). That's the term given to people we are pretty sure are believers but whose life just doesn't seem to show it. I am convinced that the term "carnal Christian" has been wrongly used. We need to get back to what the Bible says about these people.

The apostle Paul complains that the Corinthian believers could not be spoken to as spiritual. If you notice the passage carefully, he does not actually say they were not spiritual at all (because they all had the Holy Spirit), but they were in a condition that prevented them from receiving some sort of truth or being spoken to in some way. If spirituality is something like justification, which occurs as the result of faith (and I believe it is), then you can see how one could be spiritual but not show it all the time.

The Corinthians were something like the Hebrew believers to whom the writer of the Book of Hebrews wrote: "Concerning him we have much to say, and it is hard to explain, since you have become dull of hearing. For though by this time you ought to be teachers, you have need again for some one to teach you the elementary

95

principles of the oracles of God, and you have come to need milk and not solid food. For every one who partakes only of milk is not accustomed to the word of righteousness, for he is a babe. But solid food is for the mature, who because of practice have their senses trained to discern good and evil" (Heb. 5:11–14).

Now compare this with 1 Corinthians 3:1–4: "And I, brethren, could not speak to you as to spiritual men, but as to men of flesh, as to babes in Christ. I gave you milk to drink, not solid food; for you were not yet able to receive it. Indeed, even now you are not yet able, for you are still fleshly. For since there is jealousy and strife among you, are you not fleshly, and are you not walking like mere men? For when one says, 'I am of Paul,' and another, 'I am of Apollos,' are you not mere men?'"

Sounds like the same kind of people, doesn't it? A few different things are said in each passage, but essentially it seems as if we are looking at the same kind of person.

Here's a composite picture of the "carnal" or "fleshly" Christians from these two passages. They have stopped growing spiritually at a relatively early time in their Christian life, because the Hebrews passage says they should have progressed beyond the "elementary" things, and the Corinthian passage compares them to "babes in Christ." They are selfish and childish in their relationships with other believers; they love cliques and want to feel superior to others. Their comprehension of spiritual truth has become dull and their moral sensitivity has diminished. Their general lifestyle is little different from any moral unregenerate, and they may be headed for temptation to do something immoral. Paul even compares them to a person "of flesh" and "mere men," which implies that they are essentially like religious pagans. Apparently a number of characteristics that could occur in any believer temporarily have calcified into a state called "carnal," (KJV) "fleshly" (NASB) or "worldly" (NIV).

When Paul compares these Christians to people "of flesh" (a word slightly different from "fleshly" of verse 3), he is somewhat reassuring when he also compares them to "babes in Christ," which implies they are, indeed, true believers. But the Corinthians were not best described by *either* term, "men of flesh" or "babes," hence an entirely different term was required, and that was the term "fleshly" or "carnal." The ending of the Greek word literally means "characterized by the flesh," which means having the behavior of the sinful tendencies within us. In summary, their limited spiritual capacity resembled spiritual infancy, while their jealousy and strife resembled unregenerate people.

We need to be careful whom we label as "carnal." Some whom we thus classify may not be true believers and need special help to see they have been deceived into believing that they are Christians.

A PREVALENT MISCONCEPTION

The expression "babes in Christ" describes new believers, just born into the family of God through faith in Jesus Christ. Being a baby is normal; when the Corinthians were spiritual babies, they were going through a normal process of growth. The words "I gave you milk to drink, not solid food; for you were not yet able to receive it" refer to Paul's original ministry to them when they were first converted. But something had gone wrong, and that was the root of all their problems in the church. They were not yet able to receive "solid food."

Sanctification

Likewise, the Hebrews had *become* dull of hearing. New believers should not remain babies indefinitely; if they do, they are retarded, or they have suffered a relapse. Since new birth in Christ does not produce retardation, believers who seem to be babies long after their spiritual birth must have suffered a relapse.

The writer to the Hebrews was concerned about the immaturity of his readers and said that only two consequences lay before them: either they would snap out of it and go on to further growth (Heb. 6:1–3) or they would fall away (Heb. 6:4–6). If they experienced the latter, it would be impossible to "renew them again to repentance" (Heb. 6:6). Whatever that warning may mean is a matter of debate among Christians,[1] but I take it to mean that they had never been true believers and that they would fall into a state of hardness from which they would never recover.

The point I'm making here is that this teaches that one cannot remain carnal indefinitely. A lifelong state of worldliness does not exist, for a child of God will be disciplined and brought back to obedience (Heb. 12:5–13).

From a practical standpoint, think what the effect would be if one could remain in a state of carnality and still get to heaven. I know some who would be content that way. Give them the choice between the guarantees of eternal life without spirituality and eternal life with spirituality, and they'll choose the former.

Could this be the reason why the church today is often complacent? These people are being given a false sense of security based on the profession of faith they made, not based on any demands for evidence of that faith. Some critics call this "decisional Christianity" or "easy believism," neither of which I like; becoming a Christian *is* a decision and *is* believing. The issue is what is involved in this decision of faith. Is it intellectual assent to some theological facts or is it putting one's trust in Christ as Deliverer from sin?

I'm afraid that many professing believers have based their trust on a decision rather than exercising true faith that produces changes. They attend church, learn the Evangelical jargon, sometimes pay tithes, but they are no different from any other unregenerated good people.

Some people have decided it is necessary to create a special category for these Christians—carnal Christians. As long as we can enter their names on the rolls and use their money to meet the church budget, we can tolerate them. Occasionally we'll preach a "discipleship sermon" or a "make Christ the Lord of your life" exhortation in hope of getting greater involvement in our various programs. They don't respond, of course, and we chalk it up to carnality. We shake our heads and wonder why their consciences never seem to be affected, why they never meet the great and romantic challenges of vital spirituality. The tragedy is that they don't need to be challenged to greater commitment. They need to be *evangelized!* They need a warning like the one Paul gave to the Corinthians when he suggested some of them had believed "in vain" (empty belief, without sufficient basis) in an incomplete gospel without a risen, living Christ (1 Cor. 15:2).

The Corinthians who had been accused of carnality did not remain that way long, judging from the second letter. They had failed to discipline an immoral believer, and after Paul's first letter, they repented of that. In fact what Paul says in 2 Corinthians leads us to believe that they had been restored to spiritual behavior for the most part (2 Cor. 2:1–11; 7:5–13).

In addition to Hebrews 12, which teaches us that God

disciplines His unruly children to bring them to repentance and obedience, 1 John declares that although believers inevitably sin (1 John 1:8–10), they nevertheless do not "practice sin" as a way of life (1 John 3:9). Indifference to spiritual things is a symptom of the "natural" person, the unregenerate.

Other people who believe that some Christians remain carnal all their lives talk of being "saved by fire," a cliché for someone who "just makes it to heaven." The phrase comes from 1 Corinthians 3:10–15, where Paul corrects the Corinthians about what their leaders were supposed to be. A careful examination of this passage will show that people are not "saved by fire."

Paul compares the leaders at Corinth to workers on a building, and he likens himself to the "master builder" (literally, "architect") who laid the foundation. Jesus is the foundation, and the other workers are building with various materials upon that foundation. The materials represent the quality of work and how long the work will last. The gold, silver, and precious stones would be lasting efforts, while the wood, hay, and straw would be useless efforts. The day of testing comes by fire, a symbol of God's penetrating judgment, and the useless parts of the building go up in smoke, while the lasting parts remain unscathed. The workers who built with the flimsy materials lose their reward, and the workers who used the quality materials receive rewards.

The end of the comparison contains the words that have been misapplied to carnal Christians: "If any man's work is burned up, he shall suffer loss; but he himself shall be saved, yet so as through fire" (1 Cor. 3:15). Saved through fire, yet saved. This is supposed to pertain to a wasted, useless life of a nevertheless true believer.

But notice something. *Workers*, not useless Christians, are being described. These are people involved in ministry, busy people. The point of the image is not indifference but accountability for the kind of work the Lord's servants offer. Those who fail to get a reward must have flawed their work ultimately by wrong motives rather than by the kinds of behavior we examined in the description of the carnal Christian.

What kind of motives would be behind such effort? The judgment pertains to works, not carnal behavior, at least not directly. In all probability, they live moral lives, though this is not necessarily so. After examining the text carefully and considering it in light of my own knowledge and experience, I would say that these workers built for selfish, egotistical reasons. Pride of accomplishment and the praise of others motivate such people. The passage goes on to describe true leadership in the church as a servanthood to God and people. The common tendency among Christian leaders is to want preeminence and authority, to build little empires. The Corinthians were indeed treating their leaders that way, and to dispel the party spirit, Paul constructs a biblical model of leadership.

GROWING WITHOUT PAIN

Physical growth requires food. Spiritual growth, too, requires "food," but spiritual growth also demands that we must respond to the "food." If we fail to respond, the "food" becomes useless to us.

Broadly speaking, we grow spiritually as the Holy Spirit promotes our responses and obedience, using the Bible as the "food." Two problems prevent the "food" from producing growth in our character: lack of exposure to the Word and failure to apply it.

Sanctification

Ideally, we grow when we read, study, and apply the Word of God. The New Testament urges us to "long for the pure milk of the word, that by it you may grow in respect to salvation, if you have tasted the kindness of the Lord" (1 Peter 2:2–3). We grow by daily exposing ourselves to the Scriptures and systematically studying them in light of the principles of interpretation. We can learn even more if we study the Bible with a group or in a classroom. The early months of the Christian life should be a time of intense discipleship so that we can gain a comprehensive foundation in the Word of God. Best of all, if we have the opportunity, we should learn the original languages so that the vast resources of biblical reference tools in the original languages may be available to us.

An academic approach, however, has dangers. We can become afflicted with intellectual pride. Ironically, this often happens as a result of too little knowledge rather than too much. The more we are exposed to the vast knowledge of the world and the universe, the more we are humbled by what we do not know.

Prayer, especially the kind of prayer that worships God, brings about growth. As we think about who God is, we grow in our faith in Him. When we pray for others, we become less selfish, and God works in their lives by causing them to grow.

Fellowship with other believers helps us grow as we encourage and stimulate one another (Heb. 10:24–25). This happens only when we all exercise the gifts God has given us and participate together in making some contribution. If our church involvement is limited to going to hear someone preach, we will be less likely to grow. If we see our religion strictly as a personal matter, we will not grow as quickly as we would if were involved in the body life of the church.

Clarifying Basic Questions

Our biggest problem is disciplining ourselves to carry on a "devotional life." In case this term is new to you, let me explain it. Traditionally, private devotions involve spending time each day reading Scripture, meditating, and praying. Mystics and devout people have done this for as long as history has been recorded, but for the Christian, Jesus is the prime example. He often rose early in the morning to pray. Most Christians agree that the daily devotional is crucial to spiritual growth, although it also can become a useless ritual that pacifies our consciences.

We often find that our consistency in daily devotions is directly related to the pace of our lives. No doubt, sheer laziness is the greatest obstacle for some of us, but many of us simply forget because we are too occupied with other things. In the final analysis, this is a matter of values. Do we place supreme value on spiritual growth and a meaningful experience with God?

This is not a manual on the "quiet time" (as it is often called), but I have a few comments on the problem. First of all, having devotions must become a matter of discipline: you need to set aside everything else and schedule time for it. If you are undisciplined, then let this be your first objective. You have to start somewhere, for without discipline you will never please the Lord; you need discipline to deal with your sinful tendencies.

Second, if you fail in your attempt, don't quit. Ask God's forgiveness and pledge to start tomorrow. Habits require persistence, especially when it is a habit of holiness.

Third, don't put yourself in a methodical straightjacket. The time of day, length of time, and procedure are nowhere prescribed in Scripture. If someone else's approach appeals to you, use it. Don't be afraid to try something new.

Fourth, if you don't seem to be getting a "blessing" all the time, don't worry about it. Come to the time with a sincere desire to be warmed, challenged, and encouraged, but don't rely on your elusive feelings. More may be happening inwardly than you realize.

Growth requires not only food but also exercise. This is the relationship between what I have described in this chapter and what is to follow. Time with the Word of God, prayer, and fellowship provide food. Dealing with problems, trials, discipline, and responsibility force us to exercise spiritual muscles. One experience prepares us for the next.

GROWING IN TRIALS

Why is it that people who have smooth lives are often so self-centered and unpleasant, while people who suffer in some ways are kind, giving, and pleasant to be around? I know a crippled man who works hard on an editing job with a well-known magazine, goes home on the train many miles, does most of the house cleaning, cooks the meals, and cares for his wife, who is too ill herself to do all these things. He writes some of the most spiritually perceptive material I have read, is uncomplaining, and is delightful to be around. Hardship brings out either the best or the worst in people. It's the way to find out whether a person's claim to Christian faith is real. If genuine faith is there to start with, it will surely be revealed during hardship.

Paul implies that God uses hardship to reveal the strength of our faith: "And we know that God causes all things to work together for good to those who love God, to those who are called according to His purpose. . . . Who shall separate us from the love of Christ? Shall tribulation, or distress, or persecution, or famine, or nakedness, or peril, or sword? Just as it is written, 'For thy sake we are being put to death all day long; we were considered as sheep to be slaughtered.' But in all these things we overwhelmingly conquer through Him who loved us" (Rom. 8:28, 35–37).

Genuine faith stands any test. And tested we will be!

Let me suggest a point of view that may seem extremely pessimistic to you at first. God has not promised that we will always have good times. Instead, He has actually promised just the opposite: "In the world you have tribulation, but take courage; I have overcome the world" (John 16:33b). God certainly owes us nothing in the world. Are we better than the great people in the Bible and church history who have suffered? Have you ever observed how much of the Bible is written to prepare us for tribulation? Do it sometime; it may surprise you.

Some people's lives are filled with times of bitter hardship punctuated with times of relief. That they appear to be the exception to the rule is due largely to what we Westerners, especially we Americans, have become accustomed to and accepted as the norm: "good times." But our bubble may be about to burst.

The point of view I am advocating is realism, biblical realism. We should expect trials because we live in a largely corrupt, perverted world. If we have this perspective on life, it will not, surprisingly, make us pessimistic nor bitter. Instead, it will make us grateful for all things, good and bad. We'll be grateful for any good because we didn't expect it and knew we didn't deserve it. We'll be grateful for any bad because we will realize, as I am about to show, that something good will happen to our character.

James 1:2–8 describes the growth-producing role of

tribulation or trials: "Consider it all joy, my brethren, when you encounter various trials, knowing that the testing of your faith produces endurance. And let endurance have its perfect result, that you may be perfect and complete, lacking in nothing. But if any of you lacks wisdom, let him ask of God, who gives to all men generously and without reproach, and it will be given to him. But let him ask in faith without any doubting, for the one who doubts is like the surf of the sea driven and tossed by the wind. For let not that man expect that he will receive anything from the Lord, being a double-minded man, unstable in all his ways."

The "trials" described here are unexpected assaults on us from outside sources. They are not the consequences of our own mistakes or poor decisions. We may wonder why they happen, and we may even complain and question God's goodness.

The most baffling thing this passage says is that we should face our trials with joy. We can rejoice because the trial will produce something good. This sounds strange because the Bible's use of "joy" is different from our common usage. First of all, joy is not the same thing as happiness. They are closely related but not identical. The simplest way I know to distinguish between them is to say that happiness results from pleasant or desired circumstances, while joy results from a vital relationship with God. Happiness is more of an emotion, but joy can produce emotion. It's my conviction that only a believer can experience joy; any similar expression on the part of a non-Christian is merely a form of happiness.

This means that I don't have to be happy about trials, but I am able to face them with more than resignation. Instead, I can face trials with confidence, peace, and hope—this is "joy."

The key to doing this is in asking for wisdom (James 1:5). The experience of the greatest sufferer of all time, Job, leads me to think that this wisdom does not reveal why we suffer; rather it teaches us how to cope with suffering and trials. Job never learned why, but he surely asked the question often enough. In his case, Job's only problem was why God permitted his suffering. God finally convinced Job that He was the all-wise God, in full control of everything.

Some trials require decisions, and decisions require wisdom. Take, for example, the death of an elderly parent. Interment of the deceased, disposal of belongings, and the care of the surviving parent would all demand some wisdom. Some of the wisdom would be biblical, such as what the children's responsibility is to their aged parents, but most of it would be common sense. God is able to give us all the wisdom we need. As people give us advice or as ideas occur to us, we must test the advice against Scripture. But ideas will commend themselves to us if they seem to be honorable toward God and if they do not violate ethical standards.

Trials will produce growth to the extent that we look to God for wisdom to cope with them and submissively allow Him to refine our character. This passage suggests that growth takes place in a certain order. First, the testing of faith produces endurance or patience. This means that we have to exercise faith by believing God for whatever need we may have, especially believing that no matter what happens, God has a purpose. We learn one of His purposes right here in this context: spiritual growth. As we learn to trust God with our problems, He makes us patient and steadfast. We don't panic and make rash decisions, but we patiently wait until God either works it all out or gives us insight into what we should do.

Second, endurance or patience produces "perfection" and "completeness." "Perfect" here is maturity, while "complete," though a synonym, suggests the capacity to live life fully in a spiritual way.[2]

Now let's put it all together in an analogy. A worldly believer ("carnal") is consistently unspiritual in behavior; a new believer ("babe") is inconsistently spiritual in behavior; but a mature believer ("perfect" and "complete") is consistently spiritual in behavior. The mature believer consistently allows the Holy Spirit to work in his or her life. The mature Christian consistently thinks in a spiritual or biblical way, the way God thinks. This passage in James 1:2–8 informs us that trials produce this consistently spiritual behavior that is described as "perfect" (mature) and "complete."

Wisdom only comes when we ask, the passage says, "in faith." The doubter is unstable and vacillates between doubt and faith. This is called "double-mindedness." The doubter tries to live in two worlds at the same time, never giving God full confidence. This is just the opposite of endurance, the indispensable quality of active faith.

Difficult experiences in life force us to turn to God. The consistency with which we do this determines the degree of growth that takes place. As we endure trials by faith, we build more and more endurance, and this leads to maturity and completeness.

GROWING THROUGH DISCIPLINE

Have you ever been on your back in a hospital bed or faced a discouraging setback and asked the question, "Why?" In the last chapter I did not encourage the idea that we can know the "why" of our trials, but now I am going to *insist* that we know why.

Clarifying Basic Questions

What's the difference? The difference lies in the drastic difference between the purpose for trials and purpose for divine discipline. The experience could conceivably be the same: sickness, an accident, loss of a loved one, material loss, loss of a job, loss of a friend—you name it.

Hebrews 12:5–13 is the classic passage about divine discipline:

> "My son, do not regard lightly the discipline of the Lord, nor faint when you are reproved by Him; for those whom the Lord loves He disciplines, and He scourges every son whom He receives." It is for discipline that you endure; God deals with you as with sons; for what son is there whom his father does not discipline? But if you are without discipline, of which all have become partakers, then you are illegitimate children and not sons. Furthermore, we had earthly fathers to discipline us, and we respected them; shall we not much rather be subject to the Father of spirits, and live? For they disciplined us for a short time as seemed best to them, but He disciplines us for our good, that we may share His holiness. All discipline for the moment seems not to be joyful, but sorrowful; yet to those who have been trained by it, afterwards it yields the peaceful fruit of righteousness. Therefore, strengthen the hands that are weak and the knees that are feeble, and make straight paths for your feet, so that the limb that is lame may not be put out of joint, but rather be healed.

As you can see, divine discipline simply means "divine spanking." It differs from a trial in that discipline is corrective while a trial is educative. Discipline works on our faults, while trials deal with character-needs.

Let me illustrate. There's always work to be done around our house and yard. Occasionally we discipline our children for some act of disobedience by making them do some work they might not otherwise be asked to do. It interrupts their leisure time and makes them think about their offense and regret it. At other times, they may be assigned a family chore as part of their responsibility as a member of the household. Conceivably, it could be the same kind of work they were given as a punishment, but they would know the difference.

Some of you might have objections to the form of the discipline, but the illustration is clear. When we are being disciplined by God, it will probably be clear to us, for some sin will loom up before us in our consciousness. James 5:15 implies that the same kind of experience may be the result of a trial or divine discipline: ". . . The prayer offered in faith will restore the one who is sick, and the Lord will raise him up, and if he has committed sins, they will be forgiven him." Sin may or may not be the cause of the illness, but the experience of illness may be the same in either case.[3]

Discipline indirectly promotes spiritual growth. In Hebrews 12, the writer says that discipline "yields the peaceful fruit of righteousness." This is a pattern of behavior, and behavior is what spirituality is partly about. Notice also that the whole comparison to fathers and children implies growth, because family discipline is essential to growing up. Finally, the second illustration (verses 12–13) of strengthening arms and legs and resetting joints to restore lost abilities sounds like a process that restores us to growth.

Our faults and sins stand as obstacles to spiritual growth. To put it another way, sin is a detour from the path of growth. Discipline corrects us and gets us back on the way to growth.

But how does this happen? Discipline itself doesn't tell

us what is right—the Word of God does that. Discipline gets us to realize and admit mistakes. When this happens, we turn back to God for help, and He then starts working in us to bring about growth. This is another way of saying the believer frequently needs to repent.

At this point, I need to point out something we need to keep in mind so that we don't get discouraged. If we repent, we will always have a new beginning. Satan doesn't want this to happen, so he delights in convincing us that after a series of failures, God is through with us—we have somehow proven the ineffectiveness of His remedies or our inability to respond to His remedies. Keep this in mind: the Bible nevers teaches that God says to the repentant person, "Sorry, that's one failure too many. You've gone too far this time!" As long as we are willing to repent (those without hope have long passed any such desire), God is willing to forgive and start all over with us. If you question what I am saying, simply go to your concordance and examine everywhere in the Bible the word *repent* or *confess* is used. God always forgives—*always*. Our problem is that we too often are unwilling to repent.

I believe that the mark of a true believer ultimately is repentance. God uses our repentance (a characteristic of our regeneration) to bring about the remarkable phenomenon of a consistently holy life. I stress this idea because if there is a unifying concept or primary idea in my view of sanctification, it is the concept of repentance.

This idea of discipline that leads to repentance brings up the matter of sin and the meaning of forgiveness. John tells us: "But if we walk in the light as He Himself is in the light, we have fellowship with one another, and the blood of Jesus His Son cleanses us from all sin. If we say that we have no sin, we are deceiving ourselves, and the truth is not in us. If we confess our sins, He is faithful and righteous to forgive us our sins and to cleanse us from all unrighteousness. If we say that we have not sinned, we make Him a liar and His word is not in us" (1 John 1:7–10).

Note that John tells us that sin is inevitable. To say that we have no sin is a deception. It must mean sinning now, in the present, because he later refers to sinning in the past. The word "sin" is singular rather than plural ("sins"), which implies a pattern of sinning. When I use the word "inevitable," I don't mean "necessary."[4] We are always responsible for sin, because spiritual resources are always available to us if we only use them.

Sin is inevitable because of the powerful sin principle within us, the activity of Satan, and our lack of power as regenerate persons apart from the Holy Spirit. Think of it this way: sin is persistent, but God's help is available so that we can avoid sin. "Inevitable" does not mean we lose control to some irresistible force.

"Confess" means literally to "agree with God about our sin."[5] We acknowledge that we have indeed sinned against God, and that it is wrong. Notice that we confess sins (plural). Genuine confession gets to specifics; it is not content with vague generalities. This is hard to do, as any parent who has tried to get his child to admit a specific wrong knows. When we spell out our sins, we become more conscious of their sinfulness, and that reinforces our determination to abandon them. A feeling of sorrow or remorse may or may not be present, for only God produces that. The crux of the matter is agreement with God. God then forgives, not on the degree of our sorrow but on the grounds of His grace and promises to forgive.

But how can we know whether our confession or

repentance is real if we feel no deep, crushing remorse? Paul tells us that the Corinthians "were made sorrowful to the point of repentance" (2 Cor. 7:8–9). Sorrow, in this case, produced repentance. Paul had dispatched a rather hot letter to them, and they had reacted in a sorrow that Paul describes, literally, as "according to God." This either means that God Himself was responsible for the sorrow or that the sorrow was the right kind ("godly") because it led to repentance rather than bitterness. Either way, sorrow may not always be a necessary ingredient in repentance; in this particular case it was because of their hardness.

Repentance is real, then, for some other reason. Since repentance is basically a turning, it must involve a desire to change. Given enough time, perhaps a series of failures, we will decide that "things need to change," and we will allow God to change us. Confession is agreeing to let God help us deal with sin.[6] Listen to 2 Corinthians 7:11: "For behold what earnestness this very thing, this godly sorrow, has produced in you: what vindication of yourselves, what indignation, what fear, what longing, what zeal, what avenging of wrong! In everything you demonstrated your-selves to be innocent in the matter."

Let's illustrate this more specifically. Confession and forgiveness can be real without the immediate disappearance of a sin from our lives. This is especially true of sexual sins, because the sexual drive never stops entirely, even among the elderly. A man may be frustrated because he can't seem to control his lust. He feels a powerful urge when he is around certain women, or he seeks satisfaction by artificially stimulating himself whenever he experiences sexual craving. He acknowledges this problem to himself (confession), but he realistically admits that the lust may occur again. When he is tempted, he will try to become absorbed in some other activity until the time arrives when he can find release for his passion within the marriage relationship.

In summary, let's keep the air clear about this matter of discipline and confession of sin. God never gives up on believers. We can depend on Him to do whatever is necessary to bring about our repentance when we sin. If we really believe that we sin against God, we will be willing to change—or rather, to be changed.

GROWING THROUGH RESPONSIBILITY

We all find that life is full of responsibilities: responsibilities to people, responsibilities to our jobs, responsibilities to our families. Our life in the body of Christ also carries with it the responsibility to serve God, to be involved in some area of ministry. When we accept this responsibility for ministry, we have to depend on God to enable us and help us to grow through our responsibility.

Let me explain what I mean. "Serving God" often means accepting some formal position in the church. In the simple apostolic church, many roles we have come to associate with service (like ushering) were unknown. If you asked early believers about their service to God, they would have thought of some good they did for a neighbor, not of their office in the church. They would have thought of service as a way to witness to people.

Witnessing of any kind frightens us because we are not aware of all that God will do through us and for us. When we break through the fear barriers, God works through us, and we grow.

When we realize our need to depend on God in our responsibilities, we find that Scripture and prayer suddenly become much more vital and practical. Although I am a Bible and theology teacher in a Bible institute, this doesn't mean that I am always vitally concerned with everything I teach. After I received my doctorate, I taught for a few years and then accepted a pastorate. Many things I studied or taught in those early years—what makes a church grow, evangelism, pastoral counseling, and world missions— took on practical significance for me once I became a pastor. I began to read the Bible and other books from a different perspective. These things had become a matter of my personal responsibility, and in four years in the pastorate, I learned more than all of my academic years put together. I grew and I changed.

When we're busy for the Lord, we tend to pray more and in greater earnestness. We fail and start all over again. Tough decisions lead to seeking God's wisdom. All of these things produce spiritual growth.

Athletes often say, "No pain, no gain." Applied to spiritual growth, this means stretching ourselves, accepting challenging ministries in which we may doubt our qualifications, and then experiencing how the Lord makes us sufficient for them. It's my opinion that the Christian ministry is plagued by people who think they are qualified by virtue of an enormous ego or some form of training but who go about it in a self-sufficient way or full of half-baked ideas. These people are susceptible to all kinds of blunders, but the worst of it is that they are reluctant to admit the blame for failure. People don't accept responsibility unless they take responsibility for failure.

We'll grow with responsibility if we accept it both as something we can do only in God's strength and as an opportunity to serve others. The apostle John makes passing reference to a conceited person named Diotrephes, "who loves to be first among them" (3 John 9). Unfortunately, leadership places in the church often attract people with unhealthy egos, and church programs end up with irresponsible people in responsible positions.

Because we often tend to be rebellious and selfish, we perhaps should accept a responsibility that we would rather not do and likewise shun a responsibility if we hanker to do it. The former situation may stretch us and cause us to grow; the latter may merely cause our egos to grow.

DISCIPLESHIP

Spirituality is being a disciple of Jesus Christ. There is some confusion about the word "disciple" today. In its strict sense it means a "student" or "follower" of a teacher. In the Greek-Roman world, a disciple was a student of the great teachers and philosophers. Plato and Socrates had their disciples. Among the Jews, the great rabbis had their disciples, too. Paul could have been called a disciple of the great Jewish teacher Gamaliel. Likewise, the followers of Rabbi Jesus were called "disciples."

But Jesus gave the word "disciple" a special significance. Jesus demanded a commitment.[7] His disciples had to count the cost to follow Him. Let's look at several passages in which Jesus discusses discipleship.

Luke 14:25–35 is a classic discipleship passage:

> Now great multitudes were going along with Him; and He turned and said to them, "If anyone comes to Me, and does not hate his own father and mother and wife and children and brothers and sisters, yes, and even his own life, he cannot be My disciple. Whoever does not carry his own

cross and come after Me cannot be My disciple. For which one of you, when he wants to build a tower, does not first sit down and calculate the cost, to see if he has enough to complete it? Otherwise, when he has laid a foundation, and is not able to finish, all who observe it begin to ridicule him, saying, 'This man began to build and was not able to finish.' Or what king, when he sets out to meet another king in battle, will not first sit down and take counsel whether he is strong enough with ten thousand men to encounter the one coming against him with twenty thousand? Or else, while the other is still far away, he sends a delegation and asks terms of peace. So therefore, no one of you can be My disciple who does not give up all his own possessions. Therefore, salt is good; but if even salt has become tasteless, with what will it be seasoned? It is useless either for the soil or for the manure pile; it is thrown out. He who has ears to hear, let him hear."

These demands follow two parables in which Jesus makes two points: first, God accepts anyone who desires to come to Him (Luke 14:7–15); second, often the religious do not enter heaven because they really have no desire to be with God (Luke 14:16–24). Evidently this desire to be with God in heaven must be expressed by a willingness to meet Jesus' demands.

Jesus demands that His disciples must love Him more than they love their closest relatives (Luke 14:25–26). He uses a Hebrew idiom that strikingly states that they must "hate" them, an expression that means "love less." Jesus does this by showing the contrast between love for Him and love for someone on earth (see the marginal reference in the NASB; see also Gen. 29:30–31).

A disciple must "carry his own cross," an expression that probably means a willingness to make the ultimate sacrifice, if it should come to that. A person must carefully consider these demands, "counting the cost" before he or she becomes a disciple. Any other kind of following will lead to uselessness, like salt that has lost its taste and must be thrown away.

In setting forth these demands for commitment is Jesus in effect setting forth the requirements for salvation? One certainly doesn't hear such things in most modern evangelism, and many believe a distinction must be made between believing the gospel and becoming a disciple of Christ. They fear that such demands require more than the simple faith demanded for salvation and justification, a kind of good works.

They believe that the word "disciple" is used in different ways by the Gospel writers and Jesus. For example, Luke uses it in Acts as a term equivalent to "student" or "learner." Jesus, on the other hand used it of a higher level of commitment or dedication to which He challenged His followers after they had already believed in Him and become His "students."[8]

Thus "discipleship," like the "lordship" of Christ, is a later dedication of life, totally separate from the issue of salvation. In fact, some who make this distinction believe that it is the same thing as making Jesus lord of your life. What we have discussed earlier about lordship relates to this issue.

I find it impossible to interpret these discipleship passages in their contexts and plain language and see any difference between being a disciple and being a believer. Paul does not always define faith in his epistles, and he makes it clear that the works of the law cannot justify. But in the discipleship passages of the four Gospels, we have demands for commitment that are a far cry from "good works." Good works are legalistic efforts to gain God's acceptance or approval, while Jesus' discipleship demands are tokens of true allegiance—faith, we call it—to Jesus Christ Himself.

This raises a perplexing question. Are commitment and faith distinct ideas, or are they somehow related? The answer to this lies in the definition of each. Earlier, in connection with lordship, I used the word "commitment" as a decision to give one's allegiance to Jesus Christ as Master, but not necessarily a commitment to do anything. If you understand it this way, there is no contradiction with the truth of justification by faith, for such commitment is an element of faith itself.

We must be careful not to define faith merely as intellectual assent to truth. If there seems to be a contradiction between commitment and faith, it may be because we have been conditioned to think of faith in Jesus Christ as merely believing that He died for mankind on the cross; we think that believing that fact alone automatically saves us. The deficiency in such belief is that we may not necessarily put confidence in and acknowledge the kind of person Jesus Christ is. Faith and commitment are inseparable in the following statement of how to be saved: "Put your full confidence in Jesus Christ as the One who died to pay the penalty for your sins (fact) in order to deliver you from sin (commitment)." The last part of the sentence requires you to think about Christ as One who wants to change your life, and that requires a decision of commitment.

This idea is dramatically taught in the Gospel account of a "certain ruler" (a "young" man according to Matt. 19:20) who asked how to inherit eternal life, which sounds to me as if he is asking how to be saved. Jesus told him to sell his possessions, distribute them to the poor, and follow Him. This last requirement—to follow Jesus—lifts the matter far beyond mere legalistic requirements for salvation.

What was Jesus asking for? Jesus told the young man to keep the commandments, and the young man promptly replied that he already had kept the commandments all of his life. In reality, Jesus was not confusing the "salvation-by-grace-through-faith" formula, but He was getting to the heart of the matter of faith by challenging the young man to demonstrate his faith through his commitment (James takes a similar approach, challenging believers to show their faith through their "works").

Perhaps all his life the rich young man had been doing good works that had never cost him a thing. When Jesus demanded something like selling all his possessions, He got down to where the "rubber meets the road." To do that would have required James' brand of faith.

The faith of discipleship is salvation faith, and it involves a placing of one's undivided trust in Jesus Christ as the Savior from sin and the Leader of a new way of life. To say that such faith is perverted with good works is a failure to understand the nature of the commitment itself. It is not, to be accurate, a commitment to do something,[9] but a commitment or faith in Someone that *results* in doing something.

The difference between good works and the faith-commitment can be illustrated in the following way. Suppose I had a boss who asked me to do something unpleasant; I might do it because I wanted him to pay me. This would fall into the category of "good works" for a reward, a commitment for a payment. Suppose my wife asked me to do something around the house, something I also would rather not do, a job I might even consider unnecessary—and I would not get paid any money for it. But I do this job. Why? Because I love her and am committed to her. My love for her also involves faith in her (notice how John's first epistle implies this; loving God is to be demonstrated by loving others). I want to please her. This corresponds to the faith-commitment of discipleship. I do things for my Lord, because I am a believer-lover of Him and committed to Him. There's plenty of "doing," but a vast difference from the "doing" of legalistic good works, because *faith precedes the doing.*

Someone might object to this by insisting that Jesus makes His discipleship demands upon His disciples sometime after they had first merely "believed," and that, thus, they must have believed in Him without any commitment.[10] This could be answered in two ways. First, we have already seen that Jesus made discipleship demands upon people as part of the faith-requirement for salvation. Secondly, Jesus continued to make demands upon His close disciples because the challenge to discipleship goes on and on, just as the challenge to faith goes on and on. Those who truly believe will continue to meet the challenges to their commitment. Oh, of course they will resist it from time to time and will experience set-backs, but they'll come through eventually when they get tired of the status quo.

Another objection to making discipleship equivalent to salvation is that a person could abandon his or her commitment to do something, but faith in Christ is a permanent thing. Thus, discipleship and salvation cannot be different names for the same commitment.[11] This argument seems to assume that the commitment to discipleship is a commitment to *do* something rather than a commitment to *Christ Himself*. Therefore, the objection is probably not valid if the nature of faith is properly understood.[12]

We must also remember that when faith precedes doing, the doing is accomplished only with God's help. Failing to understand this causes some interpreters to be puzzled at such biblical passages as Romans 2:6–7: God will "render to every man according to his deeds: to those who by perseverance in doing good seek for glory and honor and immortality, eternal life." Those who "do good" are those with faith. The point is that God renders to every person according to deeds, but there are two kinds of deeds: those that follow faith and those that result from legalistic effort.

Jesus thought of discipleship as the most comprehensive way to describe the Christian life. His "Great Commission" to us in Matthew 28:19–20 is to "make disciples," not merely to get people to believe in (to give mental assent to) truth. He implies that disciples are made in two ways: by "baptizing" and by "teaching." Thus, a person enters upon discipleship when he or she believes (the early believers closely connected baptism with their coming to faith because it followed so closely to it), and it continues as the person is taught. Luke uses the word "disciple" to describe Jesus' stringent demands. Acts, also written by Luke, uses the word "disciple" as a term for *all* believers. Granted, some of them, like Simon the magician, seem to have proved that they were not genuine disciples later on, but this does not alter the way the word is being used.

Have you ever noticed that the word "disciple" does not appear in any of Paul's writings? Since he argued for justification by faith alone, some have assumed that he didn't require discipleship as a part of faith. For one thing, the apostle Paul created his own theological vocabulary. His word for discipleship is probably "confess Jesus as Lord" or "consider yourselves dead to sin" as the initial and subsequent steps in discipleship.

Jesus' initial requirement for discipleship was simply "follow me" (Matt. 4:18–22; 9:9; John 1:35–38). Christ's early followers apparently already knew Him to some extent before they left all to follow Him. Those who would theorize that they had previously believed and now were becoming disciples ignore the fact that Jesus gave discipleship requirements—which in reality required faith—to people who had made no such decision. The disciples first "believed" in Jesus at His first miracle at Cana, after they had committed themselves to Him in some sense by following Him. Does believing *follow* discipleship according to this particular fact? No, it simply means that their faith in Jesus had deepened and had become more specific. Since the rich young ruler was asked to follow Jesus as the crucial token of his faith as part of the discussion on inheriting eternal life, I take the terminology "follow me" as the initial evidence of inward faith that is to be continually challenged to greater and greater sacrifices as time progresses.

Look at Abraham's example of faith. Genesis 12 and 15 tell us that Abraham "believed" God, and it was reckoned to him for righteousness. He became justified by faith. Later, Genesis 22 describes the new test that comes to Abraham, and as a result of his willingness to offer up his only son, Isaac, in obedience to God's command, God strangely says to Abraham, "Now I know that you fear God, since you have not withheld your son, your only son, from Me" (Gen. 22:12b). "Fear" is an element of faith and might be better translated for our understanding as "reverence." Hadn't Abraham already "feared" God? Yes, he had, but God kept on testing this commitment to make it grow.

Our original willingness to follow Jesus Christ may not necessarily involve a clear understanding of where He will lead us, but that is not important at that stage. When trust is placed in the compelling Son of God, simple and undefined as it may be in the beginning, it is like a tiny seed that will grow into a great "oak" of refined character and faith as Jesus Christ through the Holy Spirit nurtures it. Let's suppose that a new convert who smokes cigarettes has just confessed Jesus as Lord and Savior. Must that person immediately give up smoking? Must he or she understand that as a requirement for salvation at that point? No, Jesus the Lord is satisfied that the person acknowledge His authority at that moment. Due to our society's varying views on the harmfulness of smoking, it may take time before the person realizes how this habit may be a hindrance upon his or her testimony or how it may relate to truly regarding his or her body as the "temple of the Holy Spirit."

Why make such an issue of this? What difference does it make if one makes a distinction between salvation and discipleship or salvation and lordship? Two problems lie in it. One, it can be misunderstood as meaning that we can have heaven without holiness. Two, in presenting the gospel, we may fail to get a biblical idea of what faith is all about and imagine that God is merely a great Santa Claus who likes to dispense "cheap grace"; we may never exercise the kind of faith that allows God to save us from sin and place us on the course of life that the Bible calls "discipleship."

Incidentally, I am not implying that the sincere people

who teach this distinction between salvation and discipleship are not genuine believers or effective disciples themselves. That they frequently are committed believers makes this issue complicated. I believe they take this position for several reasons. They have lived during a generation in which genuine conversions have been followed by very little spiritual growth; in short, the church has not been concerned with what we often call "discipling," that is, a concern to take converts from their profession of faith into biblical growth. This spiritual deadness has led to views of sanctification in which some sort of "second blessing" experience must take place for the sanctification process to begin.

More than this, some evangelists want to believe that people who have professed to believe in Christ are genuine believers. These evangelists may have elicited these decisions without adequately dealing with the nature of human sin. To them, confronting these people with discipleship or lordship is now the proper remedy. It could be that some of these people are coming to saving faith for the first time. In the meantime, the church has been plagued by complacency, and the watching world is unimpressed.

DECISION MAKING

Spirituality means making godly or wise decisions. It's common these days to talk about decisions as "discovering God's will." This sort of talk makes it sound as if God is keeping secrets in a game of hide-and-seek. Now if you mean by "discovering God's will" that you use biblical resources, think through circumstances, counsel with other believers, and pray for wisdom, I have no objection to it.

Sanctification

I do object to the theory of some perfect blueprint for the believer's life, because it serves very little practical use in making decisions, and it may, in fact, lead to a mystical decision on impulse or feelings, which are not always reliable guides. This is not to say that God is not sovereign or does not know the beginning from the end or has not, through His eternal decree, caused or permitted all that happens. That knowledge has the practical value of giving me confidence in the final outcome for good (Rom. 8:28), but beyond that, it doesn't help me much in my responsibility to do what honors God in my decisions.

Those who believe that their lives follow a perfect plan, which may allow for some minor deviations but which requires God providentially to step in and bring them back to the plan before they seriously go astray, probably have not thought very carefully through their theory. Take the following hypothetical situation as an example. Let's suppose that John was supposed to marry Linda in the perfect plan of God, but instead, John became infatuated with Mary and married her. (There's no biblical reason why God would step in and prevent this, or we wouldn't be warned against marrying unbelievers in 1 Corinthians 7:39 or 2 Corinthians 6:14). Now if John married Mary, he has fouled up God's perfect plan for David, who was supposed to marry Mary, not to mention Linda, who was supposed to marry John and must now marry someone else who was destined for someone else. Then who is David going to marry? Maybe this would serve as an argument for universal celibacy, but that is not God's will for everybody. If you try to solve the above dilemma by suggesting (I hope facetiously) that they each divorce the wrong spouse and remarry the correct one, I respond that that is not sufficient grounds for divorce, according to the Bible.

On the other hand, I can point to at least one instance in which God *did* want something very specific done in someone's life and intervened so that the right decision would be made. This occurred in Acts 16 when the Holy Spirit prevented the apostle Paul from his original intentions twice and finally revealed His specific will for him to go to Macedonia, which Paul and his companions decided to do. What's the point? The point is that we make the best decisions we can with the resources available to us, and we trust God to intervene in those unusual situations like the one described in Acts 16.

Good decisions are made in light of Scripture and common sense. The Bible is a "light to our path" (Ps. 119:105). It directly and indirectly contains God's perspective about many subjects; it contains all the wisdom we need in order to make sound decisions. If we go wrong, we have the comfort that "God causes all things to work together for good to those who love God, to those who are called according to His purpose" (Rom. 8:28).

So far, what I have said may bother you, because you have become convinced that there is such a thing as an individual, ideal will of God for our lives, based on passages like Romans 12:2: "And do not be conformed to this world, but be transformed by the renewing of your mind, that you may prove what the will of God is, that which is good and acceptable and perfect." This appears to be saying that with the renewed mind, we can find out what God's perfect will is for our life. The renewed mind does this by applying three "tests": what is "good," "acceptable," and "perfect." Such an interpretation is a result more of our conditioning to the idea of the individual, perfect will of God than of careful interpretation.

A better interpretation is that God has placed in His Word principles that are good, acceptable, and perfect, and on the basis of these we test all of our decisions. The will of God is already revealed in these principles, and the renewed mind is able to prove or test them in making good decisions. Such an approach creates dependence on God's Word and promotes maturity as we go about making decisions as spiritual adults and not as infants who are always told specifically what to do. This may indeed be just what Paul is saying when he compares believers to "adopted" sons who no longer are under the bondage of guardians before they receive their father's inheritance (which was called "adoption" by the Romans and the Greeks) (Gal. 4:1–7). As adopted sons they make responsible decisions toward their inheritance and are no longer told what to do every minute of the day by their tutor-guardians.

Let's see what Ephesians 5:17 says about the perfect will of God for each believer: "So then do not be foolish, but understand what the will of the Lord is." If you look at the context, you'll notice that, among other things, we are exhorted to make the most of our time (Eph. 5:16), and that sounds more like general advice. What the verse means, then, is that we understand the principles already revealed in the Bible.[13]

Someday we will all look back on our lives and discover they consist of a mix of obedience and disobedience, good decisions and poor decisions, wisdom and foolishness, although obedience will outweigh disobedience. We are free to exercise freedom of choice in a way that honors God by being in conformity with His will as expressed in Scripture. A good example of this principle of freedom under the influence of God's revealed will is found in 1 Corinthians 7:39: "A wife is bound as long as her husband lives; but if her husband is dead, she is free to be married to whom she wishes, only in the Lord." Notice the balance between regulations that God has put in Scripture and one's freedom of choice:

God's Revealed Will	Human Freedom of Choice
marry "in the Lord"	marry anyone you want to

Does this guarantee a happy marriage? Yes, if you understand "in the Lord" to mean more than merely marrying another believer (which Scripture teaches). Your attitude in your marriage is more important than the kind of person you pick. What I mean is that you should go into marriage with the intention that marriage is permanent (taught in places like Matthew 19:6 and 1 Corinthians 7:10) and that God is able to help you solve any problem that may arise (taught in such places as Philippians 4:13—"I can do all things through Him who strengthens me"). The commitment to face marriage to a specific person with all of the above factors in mind is what I call "love." This may include romantic love, and probably should, but the lasting element, or that which gives permanence to romantic love, is the deep-seated commitment.

So much for the basic principle. Just how does a spiritual person make decisions? As we have seen, the primary source of data for making decisions is the wisdom of God's Word. In studying Scripture, we come to understand in a conscious and unconscious way what the general and moral will of God is. Included in this are things like: principles of biblical ethics, God's will to evangelize the world by using us, God's will to sanctify us—everything that will glorify God.

As we face a particular choice or choices, we will quickly rule out some things in view of our understanding of God's moral will. But here's the catch: we may face several apparently good choices. Now given enough time, one or more of these may eliminate itself, assuming we can wait patiently before making the decision.

Let's go back to Acts 16:6–10 to find some helpful insights. Evidently Paul had made the decision to enter Asia, a Roman province about half the size of modern Turkey. We don't know how he made this decision, but it's safe to speculate that he carefully considered God's Word, especially the biblical mandate to evangelize the world. Beyond that, I suppose Paul thought about priorities or need, based on his knowledge of the area, plus his tendency to go to population centers where the work could more easily branch out, as indeed it did later (Acts 19:9–10).

It is fairly safe to assume that this was the process of Paul's thinking. If getting visions was the norm in apostolic decision making, I think we would see more references to visions in the course of Paul's journeys. A vision occurred at Corinth to encourage Paul, and another vision occurred during his voyage to Rome, at a time when no decision was pending. That's about the sum of them. Evidently Paul did not rely on visions to help him make decisions. Even the vision in Corinth (like the one at Troas, recorded in Acts 16) served to alter the decision he had already made. One could argue whether visions or dreams have any place outside the apostolic miracle-sign age, but I'd be content, like Paul, simply to not expect them.

Acts 16 also shows how circumstances can alter a

decision, if this was how the Holy Spirit told them not to go first into Asia and later into Bithynia. But circumstances play a larger role in situations like Paul's decision to leave Thessalonica because of the heavy persecution (Acts 17:1–10; 1 Thess. 2:13–18). We could view this as a matter of God's either opening or closing doors.

But Acts 16 has something in it that is more important than anything else we have considered so far. Paul made decisions by considering all the factors and God's ways of revealing His wisdom. After the Holy Spirit prevented Paul from entering two places and after he received the vision, Paul and his fellow missionaries jointly "concluded" that God wanted them to go to Macedonia. It is important to realize that a number of factors entered into their decision. And it will often be that way for us, too. We need to consider all the factors before we make a decision.

Let's summarize. When I make decisions, I first ask what has God revealed in His Word about His will. Next, I consider my desires. Are they worthy and wise in light of Scripture? If I delight myself in God, He gives me the desires of my heart (Ps. 37:4). Next, do my spiritual friends or other counselors have any good advice? "With those who receive counsel is wisdom" (Prov. 13:10b). Finally, do circumstances or feelings point in any direction?

Should I feel some inner peace when I have made the right decision? Possibly, for a decision that has been carefully thought through carries with it an inner satisfaction. But this is not what some people mean by "peace." They have in mind Philippians 4:6–7: "Be anxious for nothing, but in everything by prayer and supplication with thanksgiving let your requests be made known to God. And the peace of God, which surpasses all comprehension, shall guard your hearts and your minds in Christ

Jesus." This is an ideal but not an iron-clad requirement before I view my decision as good.

In the decision-making process, unworthy motives can enter my mind and confuse the issue. I am quite able, because of my sinful tendencies, to talk myself into things and feel quite good about them for a while. Thus, my decisions have to be based on factors that are more objective than inner feelings. I want the peace to confirm a good decision rather than wait to make a decision until I feel a peace about it. If I am uneasy before making a decision, it may be due to some valid danger in my subconsciousness. If the decision does not have to be made at once, I can simply postpone it, pray about it more, and more thoroughly weigh the pros and cons. If a decision has to be made immediately, I do the best I can and trust God to intervene if it is a crucial matter.

We should also examine the practice of "putting out a fleece." Gideon asked God to confirm His word that He would help him deliver Israel from its enemies (Judg. 6:36–40). I am skeptical about using such a device because Gideon was not trying to find out *what* to do. He was trying to gain encouragement in undertaking an awesome task. God condescended to him because Gideon lacked confidence.

Some people try to determine God's will by randomly opening the Bible, finding a verse that seems to point in some direction, and claiming it as God's direction. A more refined and common version of this is the practice of supporting a decision with a verse that appears to say something about the decision, even though the verse relates to an entirely different situation in the Bible. If we fail to interpret the passage in its historical context, we cannot accept the verse as valid direction.

Let me illustrate. Some people could read Matthew 10:5, "'Do not go in the way of the Gentiles, and do not enter any city of the Samaritans; but rather go to the lost sheep of the house of Israel,'" and conclude that they should engage in a ministry exclusively to Jews. Perhaps they would not go so far as to think this excluded all ministry to Gentiles, but they might conclude that the text is the exclusive voice of God to them at a decisive point in their lives. To take it this way would totally exclude the historical significance of the command and place an arbitrary meaning on it. How do these people know for sure that this is God's special word to them? Because it is found in the Bible, God's Word? To be consistent with this, they should also offer animal sacrifices, for they are commanded in the Old Testament. If they object to that, let them explain why. If they appeal to the New Testament teaching that abolishes the Old Testament sacrifices, we could respond that the Great Commission supercedes Matthew 10:5. The point is that they are actually making the same hermeneutical mistake.

But isn't all Scripture profitable? Therefore, what is the value of Matthew 10:5? Have I not made it a mere historical curiosity? The value of Matthew 10:5 (as well as a host of biblical narratives that cannot be imposed on us as valid commands today) is in the theological or spiritual *principles* it contains. One of these principles is that God was keeping His covenant arrangements with Israel by getting the message of the kingdom to them first. Movement toward the Gentile world would come later, as Paul shows in Romans 11:11–24. The personal application of this verse may be that God is faithful to His covenant promises; we can depend on Him to keep His word. Thus, the passage cannot have any bearing on a particular decision, but it serves as a general moral background for *all* my decisions.

If you apply any Scripture to yourself as part of a decision-making process, use it in a way that is faithful to the biblical context. This calls for another illustration. Moses said to the Israelites "Do not fear! Stand by and see the salvation of the LORD which He will accomplish for you today; for the Egyptians whom you have seen today, you will never see them again forever" (Exod. 14:13). What application could this have to me? The command is to refrain from any activity, especially panic, and let God do something. How or when should I obey this command? When the circumstances might be similar. Broadly speaking, the situation was hopeless from the human standpoint. The Egyptians were on one side, the mountains on the other. They could do absolutely nothing, but they might have tried to do something foolish, like attacking an overwhelmingly superior force or swimming the Red Sea.

I can think of some situations like that in my life. After I recognize that a situation is truly beyond my control, I need to consider all the available options. If no reasonable option exists, I trust God to do something, and that becomes my decision for the present time.

One last matter. Some people pray and fast when they face an important decision. Although the Bible does not command it, people in both the Old and New Testaments prayed and fasted to determine God's will. The decision to send Paul and Barnabas on the first missionary journey was preceded by worship and fasting (Acts 13:1–3). Fasting accompanied by prayer can be profitable today. Fasting helps us focus on things of God more closely by getting us out of a routine.

Chapter Five

The Right

Attitude:

We're at War!

The Warfare Mentality
The Enemy Identified
Resisting and Standing
The Spiritual Resources
Conclusion

THE WARFARE MENTALITY

Believers are in a state of spiritual warfare. If we fail to recognize this and be conscious of it day by day, we will be in danger of serious consequences.

So far in this book, we have discussed how our spiritual growth is threatened by misconceptions, sin, and weaknesses within ourselves. But threats on the outside also can destroy our spiritual lives.

Maybe this talk about war is confusing to you because you have been taught—and correctly so—that the Christian is in a state of peace with God (Rom. 5:1) and is commanded to be a peacemaker (Matt. 5:9). "If possible, so far as it depends on you," Romans 12:18 states, "be at peace with all men." The believer is to be known as a person of peace, even if we allow for bearing arms in behalf of human government in certain cases (Rom. 13:4).

Believers are in war, not in the physical world but in the spiritual realm. We see this warfare throughout Scripture. Moses confronted strange, supernatural powers in his battle with Pharaoh and the "wise men, sorcerers, and magicians of Egypt," who duplicated some of God's mighty works with their "secret arts" (Exod. 7:11). Israel was to be hostile toward the pagan religious practices, and we learn later in the Bible that this was because these pagan practices were demonic (1 Cor. 10:20). God strictly forbade any interaction with sorcery or witchcraft in the Old Testament (Deut. 18:9–13), but this was less because of their sinister nature and more because they were alternatives to God's guidance and Word.

Sanctification

An invisible warfare is taking place all around us. We find an unusual example of this in 2 Kings 6:15–19, showing that behind the outward appearance of things, spiritual forces are at work. Elisha's servant was terrified by the Syrian armies surrounding them at Dothan. Elisha prayed that his eyes would be opened to see the situation as it really was in the spiritual realm. God granted the privilege, and the servant must have been amazed at the immense number of horses and chariots of fire—God's unseen forces—that surrounded them.

Job was not aware that Satan had gone to the very throne of God to accuse him and get God's permission to afflict him. This sort of thing is part of the spiritual warfare.

We get a fleeting glimpse of this invisible hostility in the Book of Daniel. An angelic messenger comes to Daniel and says that he had been detained by opposition from the "prince of the kingdom of Persia," a spiritual being who could be subdued only by the archangel Michael (Dan. 10:10–13).

The ministry of Jesus was interspersed with encounters with demonic powers that may have become especially active in anticipation of Jesus' arrival on earth. On one occasion we learn how we must cope with these powers when, in spite the authority Jesus had given them, His disciples were unable to cast out a demon. Jesus explained, "This kind cannot come out by anything but prayer!" (Mark 9:14–29, some manuscripts add "and fasting").

But we must be careful not to blame Satan or demons for everything that goes wrong. Sometimes we get ourselves into tough spots because of selfish decisions that need to be recognized and dealt with by confession and a resolve to change. On the other hand, some difficulties—

like the trials mentioned in James 1—are used by God to promote our spiritual growth. Blaming these difficult experiences on Satan, feeling sorry for ourselves, and not accepting them as sent from God, ultimately can rob us of the good that could result from them.

People who react to trouble this way are really trying to avoid the responsibility of overcoming problems. The real attack of Satan is the way he induces us to refuse to accept our responsibility or to fail to depend on God for strength. I know a young man who believed that his temptation to look at pornography was the result of a demonic attack. He hoped to solve his problem by finding someone who could command the demon to come out so that he would lose the desire to gape at pornography. This certainly would have been easier than saying no to such fantasies in the strength of the Spirit, but it wasn't the biblical way.

What kind of power do demons have over believers? Can believers be "possessed"? In the Gospels, we read about demons who have a dominating control over certain people, and the disciples are commanded to "cast them out." The Bible never clearly says demons have to be cast out of believers. The expression "demon possession" is not an accurate translation of the biblical term that more literally means "demonize."

Many sincere Christians believe that in some cases demons can indwell believers, and they cite examples out of their own experience. In my mind, I have never been fully satisfied with two problems with the issue: Scripture never teaches that demons indwell believers; do the alleged examples of demonized believers really pertain to true believers? For one thing, some of those who claim to know of cases of believers who were demonized would assume these persons' salvation on fewer grounds than I would. A profession of faith is not sufficient grounds on which to assume, for purposes such as this, that a person is a genuine believer.

Whatever the truth about this may be, believers have the distinct advantage of the Holy Spirit's indwelling power, for "greater is He who is in you than he who is in the world" (1 John 4:4). In fact, it is the truth of the indwelling Holy Spirit that gives me a third problem with the possibility of demonization of a believer.

Note that Ephesians 6:10–20, which describes the spiritual warfare and what it involves, does not list the demon control described in the Gospels as the primary danger. Instead, we are warned against "schemes" of the Enemy rather than demonic control of our bodies and minds. Our weapons, then, are not exorcism but the resources God gives us through His death on the cross.

To have the "warfare mentality" is to be constantly aware of certain dangers and the ways to meet them. One of the ways to meet danger, paradoxically, is to recognize that, in a sense, the victory has already been won. In other words, the struggle is no struggle at all if we use the right "weapons." Through His death on the cross, Jesus left Satan powerless. Before that, Satan had the "power of death" over "those who through fear of death were subject to slavery all their lives" (Heb. 2:14–15). I doubt that this means that Satan can inflict physical death, but he takes advantage of the fact of death and brings hopeless people into bondage.

Colossians 2:14–15 makes the clearest statement of the effect of Christ's death upon Satan and his powers. Jesus dealt a decisive blow against Satan when He cancelled the legal effects of the law by satisfying its requirements. When people break the law, they die, at least in the sense of condemnation, and this gives Satan his opportunity to enslave people, as Hebrews 2 indicates. When the law's condemnation was thus cancelled, "rulers and authorities" (Satan and his demon hosts) were "disarmed." In spite of this, Satan's dominion continues to extend over those who have not applied to themselves Jesus' victory. What this means is that unless we take advantage of the benefits of this victory, certain limited dangers (short of losing our justification) still prevail.

Let me illustrate. Suppose I have just inherited a vast country estate as the result of my parents' death. Surrounding my million-dollar mansion is a six-foot fence that can easily be climbed by an intruder who might want to threaten me or steal my possessions. Realizing this, my father had installed a device that put a potent electrical charge into the fence. The device can be activated by throwing a switch. Robbers have no power over me as long as I use the switch, for I have a shield of invulnerability. But I must choose to activate the power by turning on the switch. Without activating the power, I am subject to intrusion.

The "warfare mentality" is an awareness of our defensive resources, which Paul calls the "full armor of God" (Eph. 6:11). And like the burglar device, the parts of our armor won't work for us unless we use them, until we activate their power.

For most of us, the warfare against Satanic forces is very subtle, for it attacks us through fear and complacency. I don't deny the reality of dramatic demon activity, especially in the occult and in blatant Satanic cults. Those who get involved this way do so by deliberate choice and occasionally by being members of a family in which spiritualism and witchcraft have prevailed. But Satan prefers to nullify the vitality of our spiritual life or trick us into depression and defeat. I say this, because this is the way the vast majority of Christians are afflicted.

What greater victory is there for the Enemy than to convince us that there is no threat or to confuse us about what's really wrong?

THE ENEMY IDENTIFIED

Who are our real enemies? Those who oppose our spiritual efforts or who persecute us? Paul identifies the real villains as "rulers, . . . powers, . . . world-forces of this darkness, . . . spiritual forces of wickedness in the heavenly places" (Eph. 6:12). This is surprising, because Paul could have thought of his enemies as people. Think of how he felt during his attempts to plant new churches and nurture them to spiritual maturity. On the religious side were the Judaizers, trying to confuse the issue of God's grace by requiring the keeping of the law for salvation, trailing him almost everywhere he went. On the political side were the local government officials, like Felix and Festus at Caesarea, who used him like a pawn in petty political struggles.

We need to look closely at these "rulers, powers, world-forces, and forces of wickedness." This list corresponds roughly to another list in Paul's letter to the Colossians: "For in Him all things were created, both in the heavens and earth, visible and invisible, whether thrones or dominions or rulers or authorities—all things have been created through Him and for Him" (Col. 1:16). Later, in Colossians 2:14–15, Paul tells us that Christ "disarmed the rulers and authorities" through His death on the Cross, which "cancelled . . . the debt."

It's not clear if the "dignitaries" mentioned in Colossians 1:16 are good or evil, although at least at creation they must have been good, because Genesis 1 repeatedly calls the creation "good." Many people believe that evil entered the universe through Satan's defection (described in Isa. 14:4–21 and Ezek. 28:1–19), which occurred after the original creation. This means that our real enemies are those who rebelled against God and lost their original position (see Jude 6 and 2 Pet. 2:4). This includes Satan, the leader, and a host of evil spirits, now known as demons.

The titles of these beings are arranged in a way that implies levels of authority, but I doubt this has much practical significance for us, other than the fact that they are highly organized and effective. They are dangerous, influential, and intelligent. Since they are in the spirit realm, they have a perception of reality beyond ours, giving them a decisive advantage over us, were it not for the resources Christ gave us.

How do these evil beings affect believers? For the purposes of this book, we will not discuss how they affect the world of unregenerate people, the world of sorcery, witchcraft, demon-possession, incantations, witch covens, parapsychology, poltergeists, mediums, telekenesis, and so on (although some of the phenomena associated with this part of life are pure fakery, demon powers can be real). Rather, we will examine how these enemies try to destroy our spiritual lives and how our adversary Satan, like a "roaring lion," seeks to "devour" us (1 Pet. 5:8).

These evil spiritual forces affect us by directly and indirectly applying subtle influences on us through others. These forces are behind those who oppose the gospel (1 Cor. 16:9—"many adversaries") and those who perse-

143

cute believers (1 Pet. 5:6–11—"your adversary, the devil"). It's interesting that the two Old Testament passages that may describe the fall of Satan address earthly rulers who are seen as being influenced and energized by Satan; these earthly rulers act in ways Satan would act. The future "man of lawlessness" will come "in accord with the activity of Satan, with all power and signs and false wonders, and with all the deception of wickedness . . ." (2 Thess. 2:3, 9–10).

I do not question the reality of these unseen forces. I have been engaged in Christian ministry for many years, and I have always been able to count on frustrating problems to arise whenever God's work was being accomplished. It would be hard to disregard it as bad luck or merely ordinary circumstances. Take the example of people trying desperately to overcome some sin or escape from some old way of life. It seems that obstacles occur and evil companions "come out of the woodwork" to prevent good from being realized. I know a girl who was trying to get away from the bad influences of her former way of life, even to the extent of moving to a different part of town. She finally located an apartment she could afford on her meager salary, and who do you suppose turned out to be living in the same apartment complex? You guessed it. The very girl who had dragged her down before! I've seen everything go wrong the minute a person makes a sincere resolve to obey God. What do we do in such a situation? We do what we know from Scripture is right; we don't let these obstacles or people stand in our way and discourage us. We put on the full armor of God and allow Him to turn the tide.

This great host of wicked spiritual beings pervades our world to the greatest extent. In fact, the Bible says that this world is under their dominion. Ephesians 2:2 calls Satan the "prince of the power of the air," which means that all around us in another dimension ("air") are powerful beings ruled by an evil "prince," Satan. Jesus called the Devil the "ruler of this world" (John 16:11). Paul also implies this dominion when he calls the evil beings "world-forces" (Eph. 6:12).

In spite of this, God is still sovereign. In the New Testament, Satan is described as ruling over this "age" and this "world." Most often, these particular words refer to the world-system of people under the Devil's control. Much of our culture, learning, and politics are affected. God has allowed this, and I'm not sure why. But I know that good will finally come out of it all, and God will triumph.

RESISTING AND STANDING

The believers' strategy in this spiritual warfare is surprisingly simple. We are to "take up the full armor of God" and "to resist in the evil day, and having done everything, to stand firm" (Eph. 6:13–14). The instruction to "stand firm" comes as an unexpected command. It is neither an aggressive offense nor a strategic defense. The command implies great confidence. Among the pieces of armor, only one, the sword, is an aggressive, offensive weapon.

"Stand firm" is not a command to be passive. Standing firm in the midst of attack requires courage and resolve. To use a previous illustration, we could say that standing firm against evil is like throwing the switch on the electric fence, but rather than going out to fight the intruder, you stay in your house—you stand firm.

We resist by standing firm. Any soldier will tell you that this requires great courage when it is done in the face of a terrifying enemy. This reminds me of how pioneers protected themselves against buffalo stampedes. The bravest men mounted horses and arranged themselves in the shape of a wedge between the wagon train and the oncoming herd of buffalo. The high visibility of the men on horseback firing their rifles into the air would split the herd so that the buffaloes passed harmlessly around the wagons. Can you imagine the pioneers' temptation to break ranks and flee before the stampede of these immense animals? The simple knowledge of what the herd would do under certain circumstances gave these men the courage to stand firm.

This is the nature of our strategy. We do not fight. We stand and allow God to fight for us. We apply the victory already won for us, symbolized by the pieces of armor in Ephesians 6:14–17. We do nothing that defeats Satan, but we realize what has already been done. This is "resisting."

It all makes sense. Satan is a deceiver. Thus I should expect him to create the illusion of terror or despair. If I accept this deception as a reality, I lose the battle by default. Satan only has power to the extent that I allow him to "sift" me (Luke 22:31), to manipulate me at his will. "Resist the devil," James advises, "and he will flee from you" (James 4:7).

This underscores what we already have stressed: we succeed in our spiritual life by allowing God to do His work; we are not passive, but we realize the truth and then obey biblical commands.

Look carefully at our responsibility. We "take up" and "having done everything" stand firm. The words "take up" are sometimes used in military contexts to describe the last phase of preparation before the battle begins. The words "having done everything" imply a longer process, but they essentially refer to the same thing. The picture is similar to a pilot going through a checklist before takeoff. Our checklist is a systematic realization of the effectiveness of the items of armor. When we "take up" the armor, we personally accept spiritual resources as true. When we "do everything," we become freshly aware of our spiritual invincibility in Christ.

One other phrase in Ephesians 6:13 demands our attention. We must be prepared to "resist in the evil day," referring probably to those crisis times brought on by Satan's activity. When his attack comes unexpectedly, we must be ready. Constant vigilance is in order. This is hard, because it is much easier to mobilize when a threat is apparent. But spiritual preparedness is a continual state of readiness, a costly matter as we have learned now for several decades in the "cold war" against the Soviet threat. By "costly" I mean demanding, because our tendency is to slacken, to relax, to be indifferent to moral and spiritual problems. When we do not feel the need to pray, we may need it the most. Jesus told us that we "ought at all times to pray and not to lose heart" (Luke 18:1). The illusion of peacefulness is Satan's deception.

THE SPIRITUAL RESOURCES

It is very easy to take for granted the spiritual benefits that Christ has given us through His death. Worst of all, it is easy to be careless and ignore the applications of these resources to specific situations or crises.

We have already learned that one dynamic of the spiritual life is having a proper frame of mind, learning to think according to the Spirit. Since the Holy Spirit does this by bringing the Word of God to mind, we now need to examine and plant in our minds what the Bible says about spiritual warfare.

Paul wrote his letter to the Ephesians while he was under guard, waiting for his trial to take place in Rome. He selects the armor of a Roman soldier as the most appropriate metaphor for spiritual resources, probably because of the praetorian guard chained to him twenty-four hours a day, even though it is unlikely that the guard wore all the accouterments of battle dress. Paul refers to only certain items, the more impressive ones, so that our translation, "full [or whole] armor" might really mean "splendid" or "impressive" armor.[1] Note that most of the pieces of armor are protective.

First comes the "girdle of truth." This girdle or belt was the first item to be secured in preparation for battle. The soldier gathered his long flowing garments and tied them up with the girdle so that they would not hinder his movement. The girdle gave him greater mobility. Putting on this belt symbolizes an action that must precede everything else, something that makes the use of the other items possible.

The "truth" may be Christian truth in general, but it probably has a more specific focus in the context of spiritual warfare. We may find the clue to its meaning in Ephesians 4:21, "truth in Jesus." That's a striking phrase, especially since Paul seldom used the name Jesus alone. Usually he used the title "Lord Jesus" or "Christ Jesus." The idea of truth in Jesus points to Jesus' earthly life as a pattern of truth and behavior.

When we "put on the girdle of truth," we determine not only to let God's truth penetrate our thinking but also to model our behavior, our lifestyle after Jesus Himself. When we choose to do this, we free ourselves from hindrances of the world around us, and we free ourselves to serve, for the truth sets us free (John 8:32). This preparatory step is a commitment necessary for all that follows.

Next, Paul tells us to put on the "breastplate of righteousness." It's not clear whether this righteousness is that kind we receive judicially when we first believe or whether righteousness means righteous, ethical behavior. Since this latter kind flows from the former kind, I don't think it makes much difference.

The "breastplate" was either a frontal metal piece or an elaborate scale (chain mail) that covered chest and hips. This piece covered the most vulnerable and vital area of the body—the heart. When we "put on the breastplate of righteousness," righteousness protects us from something that is the Enemy's prime target—our susceptibility to guilt.

Righteousness is God's remedy for sin, our weapon against guilt for sin that keeps occurring in our lives. We must believe that God accepts us unconditionally because of our faith in Christ's payment. God's unconditional acceptance (justification) is the basis for all of our immunity to Satan's accusations toward us. When we put on the breastplate of righteousness, we, in effect, say, "Who will bring a charge against God's elect? God is the one who justifies; who is the one who condemns? Christ Jesus is He who died, yes, rather who was raised, who is at the right hand of God, who also intercedes for us" (Rom. 8:33–34).

The problem of guilt is a major cause of mental disorders. Many modern psychologists advise their guilt-ridden clients to explain away the guilt by blaming it on something or someone in the past (like parents). Unfortunately for unbelievers, their guilt is probably well founded and can be remedied only through the Cross of Christ. A continuing sense of guilt is the result of a failure to repent or a failure to believe God's promise to forgive.

I know an elderly woman who eyes everyone suspiciously and "hears" voices that threaten to kill her. She has been diagnosed by doctors as schizophrenic and paranoid. No one seemed to know how she gradually had disintegrated to this state. She always had been rather antisocial, but then she stopped going to church because she felt people were "watching" her. One day one of her sons called his oldest brother illegitimate. Later, when the woman was asked why she had not rebuked the younger son for this comment, she replied, "Why should I? Everybody knows it is true." But everybody had not known. Then I realized what was eating away at her. Years ago, her first child had been born out of wedlock, and all this time this woman had been nursing that guilt, unwilling to face it and repent of it. She is hardened now; I do not know if she will ever repent and come to faith in Christ. That's the power of guilt, the power of an unrepentant heart.

Unwillingness to cope with guilt is similar to unwillingness to believe the gospel; the gospel is an invitation to believe what God has done rather than what we must do. Our upbringing conditions us to think that when we have done something wrong, we must make some kind of personal atonement. While it is true that we are responsible to make restitution in fractured relationships, we can make no atonement when it comes to our own guilt. We can only believe that Christ already has made atonement for our sin, and in this confidence, we can receive God's forgiveness. Justification and forgiveness are appropriated purely by faith in God's Word. When we have done this, we have put on the breastplate of righteousness.

Paul instructs the believer to put on yet another piece of armor—the boots, the "preparation of the gospel of peace." The soldier's boots were studded with sharp nails, giving him a firm grip on the ground where he stood. We see here the picture of the soldier's constant readiness to stand his ground and not be pushed off his feet as he digs his boots into the ground. And what is the preparation of the gospel of peace that gives us a similar stability? The word "preparation" means "preparedness," and we gain this preparedness through the "gospel of peace." I think that "the gospel of peace" here refers not to bringing the gospel to others, but to claiming it for ourselves. Romans 5:1 tells us that through justification, we have peace with God, we are reconciled to Him. Justification describes what God does about our sin, while reconciliation describes what God does about our broken relationship to Him because of sin. Our reconciliation or peace with God gives us stability in the spiritual warfare when our relationship to God comes under attack.

Practically, this means that though God was once offended and we were cut off from Him by our rebelliousness and violation of His law, we are now restored to Him, and He is legally free to work on our behalf. It means that God was never against us but in love provided a payment in Christ to satisfy His holy justice.[2] We were against God; we were His enemies. When we put on the "gospel of peace," we remind ourselves that a fundamental change has occurred between us and God. With this confidence, we can dismiss the inner fears that Satan plants. Sins rob us of fellowship, but this is quickly remedied by confessing our sins. Our reconciliation is permanent.

"In addition to all," Paul tells the believer to put on the "shield of faith." The shield is a protective device that is not worn but taken up, suggesting mobility. This shield was a rather large, doorlike, wooden structure bound together with iron. It protected the soldier against flaming missiles that seemed to come out of nowhere, with no warning.

Paul uses the image of flaming missiles to describe those sudden, unexpected problems or crises that upset our equilibrium. Over and above the basic assurance of our justification and reconciliation, we need that additional confidence that God is in control no matter what happens, and He will bring ultimate good out of every apparently meaningless and discouraging incident. This is a faith applied to specifics, a mobile assurance to "extinguish all the flaming missiles" of things gone wrong.

This confidence gives us the ability to "roll with the punches," to believe in a living God no matter what, to feel protected from discouragement or panic. It is interesting to note that whenever the psalmists were alarmed about difficulties or impending calamity, they never questioned God's *existence*, but they did question His *goodness*.[3]

Paul's image of the "helmet of salvation" is more difficult to interpret because our first inclination is to understand the word "salvation" in the evangelistic sense—Christ's death delivered us from sin. If we do this, it is difficult to distinguish the function of this piece of armor from all the others. We must remember that biblical writers often used words whose meanings were based on Old Testament usage. This is probably the case here with the word "salvation." For example, Isaiah 59:17 pictures the Lord Himself wearing the helmet of salvation, suggesting victory, an idea found in the more common New Testament usage. Put together, the two ideas of victory and deliverance are found in the New Testament, but in this Ephesians passage, we must limit the meaning of "salvation" to victory.

What this piece of armor is, then, is confidence in the final outcome of the spiritual warfare because of the past defeat of Satan. This helmet, this "victory mentality" protects our mind from destructive attitudes and thought patterns.

Finally Paul instructs the believer to take up the "sword of the Spirit." This is the only piece of armor that Paul interprets for us, calling it the "word of God." The word Paul uses here for "word of God" emphasizes the *spoken* word. It is the same word that Jesus used when He quoted the Scriptures to His tempter, Satan, saying that "'Man shall not live on bread alone, but on every word that proceeds out of the mouth of God'" (Matt. 4:4).

So it is the Word of God on our lips, in combative use, that is effective against Satan. This weapon verbalizes all the other weapons. It's our personal, authoritative affirmation of the truth relating to any threat or crisis.

We must consider one final weapon for spiritual warfare, a weapon that is not part of the armor. Ephesians 6:18–20 reminds us that prayer is essential to warfare. Prayer may be the means by which the resources are called into service. When crisis occurs, we pray and ask God to make our justification, reconciliation, and confidence real to us. On the one hand prayer would be the way of putting on the armor, but here prayer is more for others than for ourselves. Notice verse 18: "With all prayer and petition pray at all times in the Spirit, and with this in view, be on the alert with all perseverance." Prayer makes us alert to the needs of others, so that we help one another in the spiritual battle. Ephesians 6:19 says that we should pray for the successful ministries of others. This is an offensive strategy. Believers take ground from the Enemy when we remove more of his subjects from his kingdom.

Verse nineteen reveals an interesting perspective on the ministry of the Word. One of Satan's threats to our service of Christ is that he tempts us to make the pure gospel ineffective by adding foreign elements; in fact, removing vital elements is equally as dangerous. Paul asks believers to "pray on my behalf, that utterance may be given to me in the opening of my mouth, to make known with boldness the mystery of the gospel . . . that . . . I may speak boldly, as I ought to speak" (Eph. 6:19). Paul didn't want to be timid in the face of an intimidating enemy.

I believe the Enemy has struck at modern evangelism and the pulpit with devastating effectiveness. We have tried to formulate a message geared to our generation, but we have too often been intimidated. We have tried to avoid offense at the expense, sometimes, of the whole truth. I am alarmed by the lack of preaching about repentance and the Resurrection. I am equally alarmed by the additions of such inducements as success or happy living. These teachings totally miss the point of the gospel, namely, that mankind is alienated from God and needs forgiveness of sin.

We in the Western world simply do not see ourselves in a state of warfare. We want peace with the world, and this amounts to peace with the forces of Satan. We are unable to cope with adversity and quickly fold and compromise when things go wrong. If and when revival comes, surely it will be characterized by the people of God adorning themselves with God's magnificent armor.

CONCLUSION

Let's review the biblical methodology as a whole. Two sets of words are keys to our understanding. The first set is biblical: *sin, justification,* and *sanctification.* By *sin* is meant our tendency to resist God, to suppress truth and rebel. Knowing that we do this is crucial, because it identifies the problem.

Victory over sin starts by rediscovering the practical meaning of redemption and resurrection. Romans 6, 7, and 8 sketch for us a sort of "anatomy" of becoming holy. This involved another set of words I myself suggested: *affirm, admit,* and *allow.* In God's judicial reckoning, we died and rose again with Christ. We need to *affirm* this as a fact and act accordingly. We, therefore, no longer see ourselves as a part of the life we once lived and have repudiated. Instead, we have been "resurrected" to a new life; we are no longer dominated by sin but are free to obey righteousness.

But affirming the truth ("positive thinking") is not sufficient in itself to produce righteousness or obedience to God. Romans 7 shows how Paul's good intention did not guarantee that he would do what he knew was right. We must remember that the key to doing right is the enabling of the Holy Spirit (Romans 8). Realizing or admitting our lack of ability to do right drives us to dependence on God. Through the energizing of the Holy Spirit, as we *allow* Him to do His work, we learn to obey God. We learn to "walk in the Spirit."

But we cannot fully appreciate this truth unless we take seriously what Scripture teaches about our perverse tendencies. When we understand sin within us, we will be forced to admit that any progress in living the spiritual life will depend on the extent to which we allow God to do His work within us. Romans 1–3 teaches that our problem is even more than helplessness; it is active rebellion. The tendency to sin is normally so strong that unless we fight against it, it will win out all the time. It must be met, instead, with decisive resistance, undergirded by the consciousness that without God's help, we will fail to live righteously.

Figure 1 — Reformed (Calvinistic) View

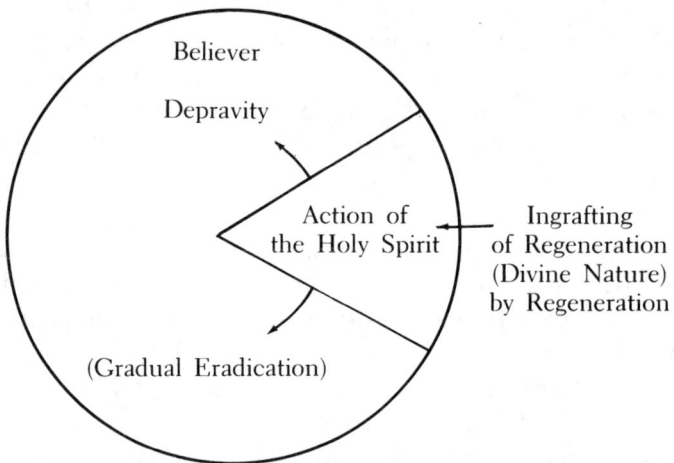

- Believer (Depraved Yet Justified)
- Indwelling Holy Spirit (Sovereignly Eradicating the Depravity)
- Result:
  Growing Holiness; Entire Holiness Never Achieved in This Life

The Right Attitude

Once we comprehend the deceptive and perverse nature of our sinful inclinations, we will realize that we need to have the supernatural power of the Holy Spirit unleashed in our lives. The Spirit Himself prods us to this yieldedness in several ways. God also uses forms of discipline to lead us to submission and repentance.

When God works within us, He writes His law on our hearts. We do not automatically obey, but His law within us produces a greater consciousness and exposure to His will.

Not only is repentance crucial to an ongoing life of fellowship with God, but it is also an identifiable quality of the true believer. Regeneration produces a desire to please God, which leads to a willingness to admit sin.

At this point I need to clarify how I interpret the biblical view of the relationship between inner sin, regeneration, and the Holy Spirit. (A detailed discussion of various views of sanctification can be found in the Appendix.) Before we are saved, we are totally dominated by sin in a condition the Bible frequently calls bondage (1 Cor. 2:14 calls it "the natural man"). Theologians often call this sinful tendency the "sin nature," but the use of the term "nature" is misleading because we also talk about "human nature," meaning the sum total of all our humanity.

The question arises: does being born again produce a "new nature" as the counterpart to the "sin nature"? The danger that lies in such theological language (the Bible does not use such terminology) is that we may be tempted to think of the sin nature as something in us that *forces* us to sin, a thing for which we are not really responsible, a scapegoat on which we can carelessly put all responsibility for our sin. I have come to prefer not to use such terminology. I believe that the two-nature theory (see figure 2), so widely accepted by Evangelicals today, is not the most accurate way to describe the relationships that have come into existence as a result of regeneration.

Figure 2 — Two-Nature View

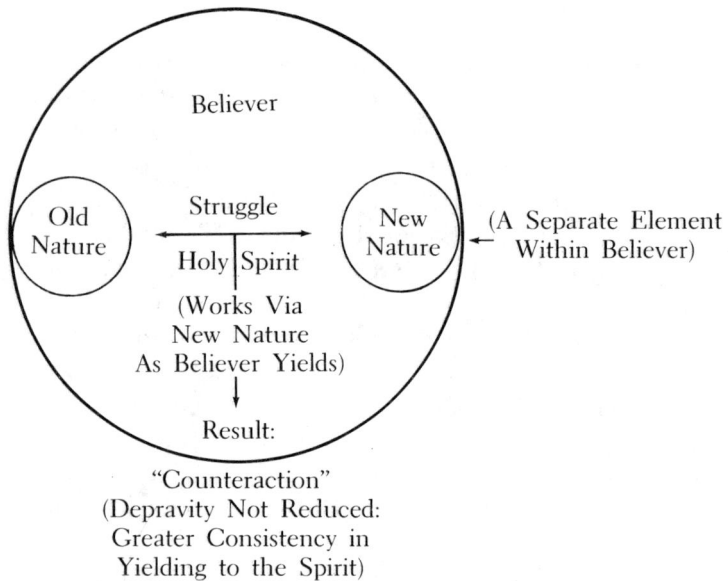

Believer

Old Nature

Struggle

Holy | Spirit

(Works Via New Nature As Believer Yields)

New Nature   (A Separate Element Within Believer)

Result:

"Counteraction"
(Depravity Not Reduced:
Greater Consistency in
Yielding to the Spirit)

Instead, I prefer to believe that when we are regenerated (see figure 3), a fundamental revitalizing takes place in our personality, which includes our mind, emotion, and will. In other words, our faculties are regenerated. Along with this regeneration of our faculties comes the indwelling presence of the Holy Spirit. Strangely, according to Romans 7:14–24, the presence of righteous desires (which Paul calls variously "I," "the law of my mind," and "the good I desire to do") is not sufficient to bring about obedience, and sin wins out to make him "wretched." We learn from Romans 8 how the Holy Spirit brings about obedience or righteousness.

Two other passages reveal insights into our situation. Galatians 5:16–17 reveals a struggle between inner sinful tendencies ("flesh") and the Holy Spirit, a struggle that must be resolved by an act of the regenerated will called "walking in the Spirit." Furthermore, 2 Corinthians 5:17 calls us "new creatures" to whom "new things" have come, while "old things" have passed away. It is insufficient to say that we have within us a new nature in light of this, as if the real "I" were neutral. We *are* new persons, the "new creatures" of Paul's epistles.

Paradoxically, though, sin still resides within this new person, and like a person changing clothes, we must "put off" the old self (the unregenerate self) and "put on" the new self, so far as our behavior is concerned, because elsewhere Paul says this "old self" is crucified (Col. 3:9–10). Even yet, our faculties are in a state of renewal (Rom. 12:1–2).

The sum of it is that we, as new persons, have within us the conflicting desires of the flesh and the Holy Spirit. As we yield to the Holy Spirit, we receive the ability to do what is according to the will of God; or as we allow sinful desires to persist, we do what is contrary to the will of God.

The ability to live a consistently righteous life requires thought patterns that can develop into patterns of righteous behavior. We must keep in mind that we have begun a new life in Christ through baptism and that we can relinquish slavery to sin and give our allegiance to Christ our Lord.

Figure 3 — Author's View

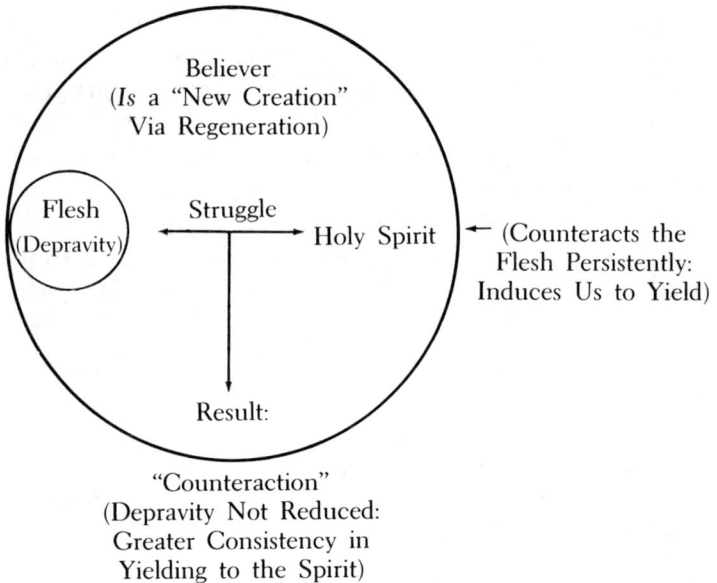

Believer
(*Is* a "New Creation"
Via Regeneration)

Flesh
(Depravity)

Struggle

Holy Spirit ← (Counteracts the Flesh Persistently: Induces Us to Yield)

Result:

"Counteraction"
(Depravity Not Reduced:
Greater Consistency in
Yielding to the Spirit)

Another major alternative to the relation of sin to righteousness in the believer is the Reformed view (see Appendix). I have tried to illustrate graphically this view in Figure 1. For more detail on the Reformed view's description of sanctification, see the Appendix.

APPENDIX: OTHER VIEWS OF SANCTIFICATION

You don't fully understand or appreciate your own view of sanctification until you have compared it with others. The heart of any theory of the spiritual life is its method of dealing with sin, its view of sanctification. We will focus on four major views: the Wesleyan view, the Reformed view, the Keswick view, and the Chaferian view. Most Protestant Christians fit roughly into one of these; Pentecostalists and other varieties of charismatics generally hold either the Wesleyan view or the Keswick view.[1]

This discussion will not only describe and evaluate each view, but it also will compare each of the four views with the view of sanctification set forth in this book. One thing all perspectives agree about: even true believers continue to sin from the moment of their salvation, although sin does not characterize their life.

THE WESLEYAN VIEW

The Wesleyan view of sanctification is also sometimes referred to as "perfectionism" or "entire sanctification" and is commonly associated with John Wesley and later with Charles Finney.[2] Simply stated, perfectionism is the conviction that it is possible to eradicate totally the sin nature within a believer's lifetime, to become totally sanctified. By "perfectionism" they mean freedom from willful, deliberate sin, not perfect knowledge or freedom from intellectual limitations. As you may expect, this belief is based on the strict interpretation of the biblical exhortations to be "perfect."

Wesley taught that this experience of entire sanctification could be instantaneously acquired by a decisive act of faith, but it is separated from conversion by an interval and thus often referred to as a "second act of grace" or a "second blessing." Wesley explained that believers would not be free from "errors and faults," but they would be so fully motivated by love for God that they would avoid "voluntary sin."[3]

Modern perfectionists tend to view sanctification as a result of a longer process, not an instantaneous result of a crisis.[4] Some people who hold to this view claim they have not sinned since they achieved their total sanctification, but neither Wesley nor Finney made such claims. In fact, Wesley and Finney would have considered such claims as self-serving and possibly a "stumbling block to the church."[5]

Could one maintain this state of perfection for the rest of his or her life? Theoretically, yes. It is interesting, however, that Wesley taught that people could fall from their state of sanctification. With this in mind, his view is not all that different from those who believe that relatively high levels of sanctification can be reached with lapses into disobedience that require restoration.

Perfectionism is based on those biblical texts that command holiness and perfection. But when it came to such passages as 1 John 3:9, "No one who is born of God practices sin," even John Wesley had to admit that new believers should not see this as a demand for sinless perfection, but rather an ideal to be sought.[6]

The major problem with perfectionism is found in its

attempt to make a distinction between sin committed before a person's entire sanctification and the "errors" committed after the entire sanctification. This artificial distinction soft-pedals the sinfulness of the inner person's tendencies, whether or not these tendencies reach the stage of actions. In other words, this view does not do justice to sin when it occurs at the stage of inner lust. Furthermore, perfectionism hedges in its definition of holiness. Wesley and Finney were too honest to lay claim to being perfect, but they wanted to hold perfection up as a possibility to provide adequate incentive toward holy living. *(Standard/Goal)*

Perfectionism also fails to take seriously the biblical passages that describe the struggle between the flesh and the Spirit and which never say that such struggle eventually will come to an end. The perfectionists regard Romans 7 as the experience of an unregenerate person trying to keep the law, but their exegesis of such a passage is not always careful. Also, they fail to take into account that Paul describes as "perfect" (some versions translate it "mature," but the word is "perfect") those who *strive* for the goal of "perfection" (Phil. 3:15).

THE KESWICK VIEW

Keswick (the "w" is silent) teaching, like perfectionism, looks at sanctification ("victorious life") as a separate, crisis experience, distinct from salvation or justification.[7] They will agree that sanctification begins in some sense at the time of justification, because of the gift of the Holy Spirit. Sanctification begins "in real earnest"[8] by a crisis also called the "second blessing."

This crisis involves an exercise of faith in which

sanctification, like justification, is received as a gift. Up to this point, Keswick teaching looks remarkably like Wesleyanism, but, unlike Wesleyanism, Keswick teaching denies that sin can be totally eradicated.

The heart of Keswick doctrine is its belief that faith is the key to deliverance from sin. This deliverance does not come with struggle or painful effort or earnest resolution and self-denial but "by [a handing] over of the fleshly deeds of the body to the Spirit for mortification,"[9] an act of pure faith, so that "it is the Holy Spirit's responsibility to do the rest.[10] This "appeal to the Spirit" assures instantaneous victory. The key phrase among Keswick followers is "let go and let God."

Another typical approach is their heavy reliance on Romans 6–8, with their interpretation of its commands as acts of once-for-all faith in this crisis experience. Victory over sin is found in the words, "reckon yourselves dead," "present" (once-for-all), and in identifying oneself with Christ's victory at the Cross in an act of faith. The struggle described in Romans 7 is understood as a person's abnormal, relatively fruitless effort to deal with his or her own sin; Romans 8 describes the victory in the Spirit that results from a person's act of faith in Christ.

There's nothing wrong with doing things in faith. This is obviously part of the prescription for success in the view I advocate. But there is a lack of attention to another obvious biblical command: to trust this enabling while at the same time entering into those acts of obedience and self-denial—God's work in concert with our obedience. Such an incomplete concept is known as "quietism"[11] or "passivism."[12]

According to the Keswick view, a state of reduced struggle is gained once the gift of sanctification has been appropriated, a high plane of victory in which one has discovered and more readily implements faith as its method of victory. The experience described in Romans 7 is a frustration to be left behind. To put it another way, the Keswick view does not perceive realistically the pernicious and persistent nature of indwelling sin. It must be discouraging to those who have considered the sin nature largely subdued only to discover to their dismay that it is still quite active.

THE REFORMED VIEW

The Reformed view is taught by those who trace their theological roots back to the second-generation reformer John Calvin.[13] A simple description of this view is "irresistible sovereignty."[14] According to the Reformed view, sanctification begins at the moment of justification and continues in a gradual "eradication" or "extermination" of depravity by the Holy Spirit, a process that will never be complete until death. Thus, entire sanctification never takes place in this life.

The Reformed view does not deny human activity, but it teaches that God irresistibly induces the human will to obey, emphasizing divine sovereignty, which is characteristic of Reformed theology as a whole. The following quotations describe this point of view:

> Sanctification is a work of God, the continuance and completion of which He Himself undertakes and guarantees (1 Thess. 5:23–4; 1 Cor. 1: 8–9), but He performs it by eliciting the active participation of its subjects.[15]

> Sanctification is not partly the work of God and partly the work of man. . . . God effects the work in part through the

instrumentality of man as a rational being, by requiring of him prayerful and intelligent cooperation with the Spirit.[16]

When we are called to speak, act, or fight, we do so as though we were doing it all ourselves, not perceiving that it is Another who works in us both to will and to do.[17]

The Reformed view also holds that the believer's will continues to be depraved,[18] although the Holy Spirit gradually reduces this depravity and renews the will. The Spirit must induce the will to choose good. When we obey God's commandments, we make decisions, but the reality of the matter is that the Holy Spirit has brought it about. We should not think that we can will on our own to do good, for that would be a form of the ancient heresy called Pelagianism.[19]

It is common, though not entirely fair, to read Reformed writings and conclude that their authors think we're all mere robots. It's my opinion that their frequent failure to show how we actually get involved with our own actions, will, and desires contributes to this impression. A delicate balance needs to be maintained when describing how God works and how men and women work. I believe in the ultimate, sovereign success of God's work in us, but I also believe in the necessity of our responsible choices. Many Reformed writers would agree with this, but an emphasis on the divine side of activity is characteristic of much of Reformed thinking.

I am bothered by the use of the term "eradication." One would think that unless sin within us is of an infinite quantity, the gradual removal of it would be complete in some of us, at least. I can't find much biblical basis for the principle of reduction of sin itself, but I can see the reduction of sinful behavior. Sin, to use an analogy, must be pinned to the canvas, but the possibility of its rearing up when we relax our moral strength and exerting tremendous strength even later in our life is possible. Is sanctification a gradual eradication of sin or a gradual ascendancy of the Holy Spirit?

The Reformed view rejects the concept of two natures. Instead, regeneration brings about an "ingrafting" of a new life-principle into the sinful, depraved human nature. The Holy Spirit gradually increases the new life-principle and gradually reduces sin. This view prevents a misunderstanding characteristic of those who believe in the old nature and the new nature: that somehow the believer is really two persons and can blame something other than himself or herself for personal sin.

The great strength of the Reformed view is that it insists on the process of sanctification from the time of salvation, an extension of the work of initial regeneration, and an evidence of true faith.

THE CHAFERIAN VIEW

Lewis Sperry Chafer, the first president of Dallas Theological Seminary, has provided another alternative view of sanctification.[20] Chafer teaches that the two natures—the old and the new—struggle within us, and when we continually yield to the Holy Spirit, the struggle is resolved, sin is defeated, and obedience and spiritual growth take place.

Chafer's view is similar to the Keswick at some points. For instance, sanctification begins, for all practical purposes, when a crisis experience occurs when we dedicate ourselves to Jesus Christ as our Lord. At this time we discover the futility of our self-effort, and we allow Jesus to be Lord over every area of life. It's a "once-for-all" event, like the Keswick teaching, a conclusion that rests on the aorist tense of the commands "present" in Romans 6:13 and 12:1 (see note 3, pp. 173–75).

Chafer teaches that before we make this dedication, and this would include the idea of discipleship, we are "carnal" or "babes," though Chafer, unlike more recent writers, taught that it was possible and even preferable for such dedication to occur at the time of salvation.[21] Later writers, in their desire to avoid the danger of good works in salvation, have stressed that faith in Christ as Savior is entirely distinct from dedication to Christ as Lord.[22]

When Chafer and others place a period of time between justification and sanctification and identify the "carnal" Christian as a "babe" in Christ, they tend to give the status of "normal" to being carnal. The carnal Christian is saved and has the indwelling Holy Spirit, but true spirituality requires one to be properly "adjusted" to the Holy Spirit beginning with dedication.

Sin, according to the Chaferian view, is dealt with by a process called "counteraction,"[23] the new nature against the old or the Spirit against the flesh, a process involving the filling of the Spirit. The old nature is never fully eradicated, but greater consistency is achieved although conflict never totally ceases.

The major flaw in the Chaferian view is its separation, not only in principle, but in time, between justification and sanctification. They teach, however, that justification and sanctification are "inseparable,"[24] so that it would not be accurate to say one could get to heaven without sanctification. True believers will sooner or later dedicate themselves. Nevertheless, it is common for some to construe the view as teaching that believers could be "carnal" or in a state of sin all their lives and still be regarded as true believers.[25]

Frankly, I believe the Chaferian view of dedication is not founded on the teaching of Scripture but is an attempt to explain how many "believers" can be indifferent to the things of God. Furthermore, the idea of a once-for-all dedication is not grammatically acceptable or true to biblical teaching on the nature of the believer's sin. When it comes to sin, decisions need to be repeated, no matter how dramatic they may be. The sin nature is simply too persistent. I will admit that some people have had unusual experiences that have profoundly changed their lives, but the Bible does not require this as a norm.

CONCLUSION

The view of sanctification that I have set forth in this book is probably closer to the Reformed view than to any other. I have taken exception to its concept of the never-completed eradication of sin and prefer to view the gradual ascendancy of the Holy Spirit as a more logical explanation of how sin is gradually diminished in our behavior.

I also believe that regeneration has had a more drastic effect upon our faculties, even though they are being renewed gradually, so that we fundamentally desire to please God. Our failure to do so is better explained by the fact that sin within us tends to dominate unless we decisively yield to the Holy Spirit.

I hold to the sovereignty of God in sanctification, but I also believe that we are expected to exert moral effort to please God. In my view, the actions described in Romans 6:13 and 12:1 are continuous, decisive resolves to yield to the Holy Spirit. Once repentance and lordship are properly defined, the Chaferian distinction between salvation and lordship may no longer be necessary.

We must make responsible choices of faith, and in this I agree with the Keswick emphasis on faith in sanctification. But I try to avoid "passivism" by demanding that believers act in dependence upon the Holy Spirit.

Each of the views that I have compared has some elements of truth because all are attempts to interpret Scripture. If you were to study the lives of those within each system, you would find it difficult to say that one group has more of a corner on holiness and spirituality. If any single view deviates from what the Bible teaches, it can lead the believer into problems and possible sidetracking from spiritual growth. We must try to be faithful to Scripture in our own view, for it will lead to greater consistency in the Christian life.

Appendix: Other Views of Sanctification

VIEWS OF SANCTIFICATION COMPARED

	Nature of justifying faith	Time Sanctification Begins	Dynamics of Sanctification	Process of Sanctification
Wesleyan	Jesus: Savior; First act of grace	Later than justification; second act of grace; undesirable struggle precedes	Decisive act of faith; often filling or "baptism of Spirit"	Little or none; attained perfectly at the point of decisive faith; might be lost; human "faults" linger; "perfect love" controls and sin is totally eradicated.
Keswick	Jesus: Savior; "First blessing"	Later than justification; second blessing; undesirable struggle precedes with sin nature.	Decisive act of faith; "let go and let God"; "once-for-all"; Holy Spirit takes full control.	Relatively less struggle, even at first; rededications probably necessary; high level of living by faith; sin nature subdued.

Sanctification

	Nature of justifying faith	Time Sanctification Begins	Dynamics of Sanctification	Process of Sanctification
Reformed	Jesus: Savior and Lord ("lord" = confession as master)	Immediately following justification	Sovereign, gradual change by indwelling Holy Spirit who works within to make believer want to obey.	Gradual "eradication" of sinful tendencies ("depravity"); eradication never complete in this life.
Chaferian	Jesus: Savior and Lord ("lord" = deity only)	Later than justification, when believer realizes personal need	Make Christ Lord "once-for-all" (dedication); followed by "counteraction" between old and new natures via Spirit	Gradual growth in consistent holiness; reaffirmation of original dedication; sin nature never eradicated in this life.
Author	Jesus: Savior and Lord ("lord" = "master" as a confession)	Immediately following justification	Sovereign, gradual change by indwelling Holy Spirit who induces us to obey and energizes our efforts	Gradual ascendancy of Spirit over continuing sinful tendencies; continual rededication of decisiveness.

NOTES

Chapter One

[1]P. V. George, *Young India*, 473, as quoted in *The Unique Christ and The Mystic Gandhi* (Travancore, India: The Malabar Christian Office, 1933), 149.

Chapter Two

[1]Some denominations (Lutherans, for example) believe that a person actually is regenerated and endowed with the Holy Spirit at the time of water baptism.

[2]It is possible that the Pauline terms *ton palaion anthropon* (the old self) and *ton neon anthropon* (the new self) are actually references to Adam and Christ respectively, since Paul describes our relation to each as "in Adam" or "in Christ." See Markus Barth, *Ephesians*, Vol. II in the *Anchor Bible* (Garden City, New York: Doubleday & Company, Inc.), 537–40.

[3]Thus Charles Ryrie (*Balancing the Christian Life* [Chicago: Moody Press, 1969], 79) builds his basic concept of sanctification on the view that Romans 12:1 is a "single, irrevocable act of surrender." For refutation of this view of the significance of the aorist tense, see Frank Stagg, "The Abused Aorist," *Journal of Biblical Literature*, 91:222–31; and Charles R. Smith, "Errant Aorist Interpreters," *Grace Theological Journal*, (Fall, 1981): 105–226. Smith writes: "Ryrie builds a theological point on the aorists of Rom. 6:13b and 12:1. . . . Walvoord makes the same error. . . . But neither grammar nor theology suggests any such limitation on these verbs. . . . Is it dishonoring for a Christian who has failed (as all do) to present himself anew? (In reality, as long as men are sinners, no presentation can be a once-for-all presentation!) But frequency is not the point. Only the *fact* of presentation is at issue."

Sanctification

Commentators generally do not agree about the significance of the aorist imperative contrasted here with the present imperative, though most agree that the present suggests *continuous* action. Murray (*Epistle to the Romans* in *The New International Commentary on the New Testament* [Grand Rapids: Wm. B. Eerdmans Publishing Company, 1959], 228) calls it a "once-for-all" act and so does Hodge (*Commentary on the Epistle to the Romans* [Grand Rapids: Wm. B. Eerdmans Publishing Company, 1947], 205), but this cannot be sustained purely on the basis of the aorist itself. Meyer (*The Epistle of Paul to the Romans* [New York: Funk and Wagnalls, 1884], 241–42) prefers the idea of instantaneousness and climactic action. Godet (*Commentary on Romans* [Grand Rapids: Kregel Publications, 1977], 251) suggests "to accomplish without delay." Lenski (*The Interpretation of St. Paul's Epistle to the Romans* [Wartburg, 1945], 415) says "definitely present yourselves to God." Cranfield (*Commentary on Romans* in *The International Critical Commentary* [Edinburgh: T. & T. Clark, 1978], 1:305) sees it as a "contrast" at the beginning with the old way of life. Hendricksen (*Romans* [Grand Rapids: Baker Book House, 1980], 202) says "consecration to God must be personal, wholehearted." Barth, (*The Epistle to the Romans* [Oxford, 1933], 211) suggests "an existential presentation to God." H.C.G. Moule (*The Epistle to the Romans* [London: Pickering and Inglis, n.d.], 168) suggests that it is a critical resolve, a decision of surrender. Sanday and Headlam (*The Epistle to the Romans* in *The International Critical Commentary* [Edinburgh: T. & T. Clark, 1902], 161) says "dedicate by one decisive act, one resolute effort" and thereby appears to agree with Murray in his use of "one." Lange (*Romans* in *Commentary on the Holy Scriptures* [Grand Rapids: Zondervan Publishing House, n.d.], 210) agrees with H. Schmidt, "The imperative present commands to occupy one's self with something; the imperative aorist, to accomplish something."

174

Notes

In summary, the weight of the authorities seems to favor the idea of decisiveness or resolve as contrasted to habitual practice in the relation between "go on presenting" and "present" (aorist). According to grammarians the aorist intrinsically makes no reference to the *kind* of action, merely to the *fact* of the action. The context determines the meaning.

[4]Ryrie (*Balancing the Christian Life*, 169–81) argues that the issue of lordship necessarily must be distinct from saviorhood because one can "fall away" from "commitment" and this would imply falling away from faith, too, if commitment to lordship is a part of believing Jesus is Savior. Several answers occur to me regarding this objection to lordship at salvation. I have defined lordship at salvation as a recognition of the authority or sovereignty of Christ, separate from a commitment to carry out its implications in decisions to do certain things as a result of it. A person could "fall away" temporarily from a commitment to do something without consciously defecting from his or her faith or commitment to Jesus' lordship. Furthermore, it is not clear to me what Ryrie means by "falling away." If he means a total loss of faith, I would agree that a true believer will never fall away from faith, and this would include commitment to Jesus' authority or lordship. What is possible, however, is a temporary "lapse" of faith and commitment, or better yet, a temporary "eclipse" of such faith and commitment. As a biblical example, I would cite the case of the apostle Peter who clearly declared his faith in Matthew 16 and later lapsed from it during the trial and crucifixion, only to be restored to it at the Resurrection. Bear in mind also that Ryrie views lordship as allowing Christ to be "lord over one's life," an expression that means that we consciously turn over our lives in terms of specifics to Christ's control. I have defined lordship as an objective commitment to Christ's sovereign authority as God at the time of conversion and the carrying out of the implications of this in the specifics as part of sanctification, the subjective aspect of lordship.

[5]Charles Hodge (*Commentary on the Epistle to the Romans*, 341) says: "This confession, therefore, includes in it an acknowledgment of Christ's universal sovereignty, and a sincere recognition of his authority over us." John Murray (*The Epistle to the Romans* [Grand Rapids: Wm. B. Eerdmans Publishing Company, 1959) II, 55: "The confession, 'Jesus as Lord,' or 'Jesus is Lord' refers to the lordship that Jesus exercises in virtue of His exaltation . . . His investiture with universal dominion." Everett Harrison (*Romans* in the *Expositor's Bible Commentary* [Grand Rapids: Zondervan Publishing House, 1976), 112) cautions: "Paul's statement . . . is misunderstood when it is made to support the claim that one cannot be saved unless he makes Jesus the Lord of his life by a personal commitment . . . Paul is speaking of the objective lordship of Christ. . . ." With this I partly agree. Lordship at salvation is not a knowledgeable surrender of specific items or areas of our life (subjective) but a recognition of Jesus' lordship authority (objective). But I disagree with Harrison's remark about a "personal commitment," although such language is probably subject to clarification. F. F. Bruce (*The Epistle of Paul to the Romans* in *The Tyndale New Testament Commentaries* [Grand Rapids: Wm. B. Eerdmans Publishing Company, 1963], 205] says: ". . . acknowledgment of the supreme honour to which God has exalted Him. . . ." H. Bietenhard ("Lord," *The New International Dictionary of New Testament Theology,* Vol. II [Grand Rapids: Zondervan Publishing House, 1975], 514) sees it as a confessional cry. "With this call the New Testament community submitted itself to its Lord, but at the same time it also confessed Him as ruler of the world. . . ."

[6]Charles Ryrie (*Ryrie Study Bible,* note on Acts 2:38, 1648) interprets "repent" as a changing of one's mind, "specifically, here, about Jesus of Nazareth. . . ." Later, ("Synopsis of Bible Doctrine," 1950) he describes repentance as "a valid condition for salvation when understood as a synonym for faith." Ryrie regards repentance a false addition to faith "when understood as

a prerequisite, requiring the cleansing of the life in order to be saved." I agree with this latter statement but consider his definition of repentance in Acts 2:38 as a "change of mind about Jesus Christ" as unfounded and arbitrary in light of the word's normal usage. Furthermore, repentance indeed is often used interchangeably with faith, but it is not a "synonym" for faith. Rather, each is an aspect of one single decision we call "conversion," so that frequently one stands for the other. Ryrie is carrying his definition of repentance a step further than his former teacher, Lewis Sperry Chafer (*Systematic Theology*, Vol. III [Dallas: Dallas Seminary Press, 1948], 372–78), who carefully avoids describing repentance as a change of mind in reference to sin. Chafer calls it a turning from "other confidences" to trust in Christ, a virtual synonym for believing. Chafer begins with an effort to remove sorrow for sin as a condition for salvation, though he admits sorrow might lead to repentance. But before he is through, it is not clear whether repentance for sin has anything to do with repentance at conversion.

[7]"Repentance" and "repent" usually refer to sin in both the Old and New Testaments, though occasionally they refer to a turning or change of mind in reference to something else. The Hebrew word *shub* simply means "to turn" or "to return," but its most important theological use is the sense of turning away from evil (Victor P. Hamilton, "shub," *Theological Wordbook of the Old Testament*, Vol. II, 909). The New Testament word *metanoia* is closely related to the Hebrew concept, so that the literal meaning, "change of mind" is less intellectual and more a matter of will or decision, thus a turning from something. Another term meaning "to repent," *epistrepho*, emphasizes turning to God, while *metanoeo* (from *metanoia*) emphasizes turning from evil (J. Geotzmann, "metanoia," *The New International Dictionary of New Testament Theology*, Vol. I, 357–58).

[8]See Acts 2:38; 3:19; 8:22; 17:30; 26:20. Chafer argues that the relative absence of the term "repent" in Romans and John's

gospel shows that a separate act of repentance is not a requirement of salvation (*Systematic Theology*, Vol. III, 376). While this is true, if repentance is defined as sorrow for sin or cleansing of the life, the usage in Romans and John does not prove it. Otherwise the passages in Acts and Revelation pertaining to unbelievers (where only "repent" occurs) would imply that *believing* as a separate act is not required. It is better to view "repentance" as implying belief and "believing" as implying repentance.

[9]The standard theologies are virtually unanimous on this. A. H. Strong, (*Systematic Theology* [Philadelphia: The Judson Press, 1907], 832, 835–36) defines repentance as "that voluntary change in the mind of the sinner in which he turns from sin." Further, "true repentance . . . never exists except in conjunction with faith . . ." and again, ". . . wherever there is true faith, there is true repentance." Louis Berkhof (*Systematic Theology* [Grand Rapids: Wm. B. Eerdmans Publishing Company, 1941], 486–87) agrees: Repentance is ". . . that change wrought in the conscious life of the sinner, by which he turns away from sin." He adds, ". . . true repentance never exists except in conjunction with faith. . . . The two are but different aspects of the same turning,—a turning away from sin toward the direction of God." William G. T. Shedd (*Dogmatic Theology*, Vol. II, 535) is more precise in his definition of *metanoia* as a "change of mind" in the sense of "disposition, will, or inclination." He also agrees that "faith and repentance are inseparable and simultaneous." Like John Calvin (*Institutes of the Christian Religion*, [Philadelphia: Westminster Press, 1955], III, 3, 5), he believes that faith precedes repentance in a logical sense. Perhaps one of the simplest and most accurate definitions of repentance is found in *The New Scofield Reference Bible*, 1911: "Repent is used in the New Testament to indicate a change of mind in respect to sin, God, and self. . . . Repentance is not an act separate from faith, but saving faith includes and implies that change of mind which is called repentance. . . ."

Notes

[10]Commentators differ about whom Paul is describing in Rom. 7:7–13. Some say:

(1) Paul is speaking autobiographically of some time before his conversion, perhaps his youth. This view faces the problem of the words, "apart from law," which seems strange to a person raised in a Jewish home.

(2) Paul speaks as a typical Jew. This view suffers from the same problem.

(3) Paul speaks as if he were Adam. This view has a problem with the apparently personal reference to the sin of coveting, which is difficult to apply to Adam.

(4) Paul speaks in the name of the Jewish people as a whole. The personal reference is forced here, too.

(5) Paul speaks for mankind as a whole. While commending itself because of Paul's apparent attempt to say something meaningful to all people, the personal reference is still somewhat of a problem.

[11]How could Paul as a regenerated believer say, "I am of flesh, sold into bondage to sin"? The term "of flesh" means "constituted" by the flesh, and is slightly different in form to the term "fleshly" ("carnal" KJV), which Paul clearly applies to believers in 1 Corinthians 3:3. Cranfield believes that Paul uses the phrase "of flesh" here to mean that in a qualified sense, the believer has something in him or her opposed to God but not to the same extent that the unbeliever is opposed to God (357). The words "sold under sin" are even more difficult to apply to the believer, but "they bring out forcefully an aspect of the Christian life that we gloss over to our undoing. When Christians fail to take account of the fact that they . . . are still 'sold under sin,' they are specially dangerous both to others and to themselves because they are self-deceived" (Cranfield, *Commentary on Romans*, 358).

Chapter Three

[1]Exegetes often recognize the words "be filled with the Spirit" as metaphorical, but the standard lexicons generally make no reference to this use of the Greek verb *pleroo* or to Ephesians 5:18 specifically. Luke, both in his Gospel and in Acts, uses the synonym *pimplemi* to refer to the filling of the Spirit. Jesus, for example, was "full" of the Spirit before His temptation (Luke 4:1), and early believers were "filled" with the Spirit so they could speak the Word boldly and speak in "other tongues" (Acts 2:4). On the other hand, Ananias was "filled" in his heart by Satan (Acts 5:3) to commit the sin of deception. I believe Paul has essentially the same metaphorical use in mind in Ephesians 5:18, especially in light of his comparison with drunkenness by wine, where the point of comparison is doing what is normally contrary to one's inclinations or abilities. I agree with Marcus Barth (*Ephesians* in the *Anchor Bible*, 34A, 582): ". . . it may be that the formula . . . 'in the Spirit' dominates the verb 'be filled' so completely as to give it a metaphorical sense. Therefore 5:18 may mean 'be filled' (or 'be perfect') . . . in the spiritual sphere (that is, in a Spirit-directed conduct). . . ."

[2]Arndt and Gingrich (*A Greek-English Lexicon of the New Testament*, s.v. "pneumatikas," 685) define the word in the great majority of cases as "caused by or filled with the (divine) Spirit, pertaining or corresponding to the (divine) Spirit."

[3]Some scholars, like Lewis Sperry Chafer (*He That Is Spiritual* [Grand Rapids: Zondervan Publishing House, 1967], 15–22), teach that saved people are not spiritual until they have been "adjusted" to the Holy Spirit. They can be "saved" and have the Holy Spirit, but they must opt for the next category of being spiritual. This conclusion possibly arises out of Paul's telling the Corinthians that he could not speak to them as to spiritual people. This may not necessarily imply that they were not "spiritual" in some sense, merely that they could not be *treated* as spiritual. First Corinthians 2:10 teaches that all believers have the Holy Spirit and that He reveals the things of

God to all believers (note Paul's inclusive idea in his use of "us"). The danger that lurks in Chafer's concept is the notion that believers can remain, through their indifference, in a state of perpetual carnality, though Chafer apparently did not teach this. I deal with this misconception in the first part of chapter 4.

Chapter Four

[1]Though interpretations of Hebrews 6:4 vary among exegetes, most would agree that the writer's point is that believers must press on to maturity. One other popular view is that if believers do not mature, they will "fall away" and be recovered by usefulness only through severe discipline (symbolized by the burned field in 6:7–8). I prefer the interpretation in which only true believers ultimately will press on to maturity. Those who fall away are not true believers at all, and due to their greater enlightenment, they are irretrievable. The major problem with my view is in explaining how such unregenerate people could be described as "partakers of the Holy Spirit" (Heb. 6:4). This problem could be alleviated by recognizing the covenant mentality of the Hebrew readers who could conceive of a corporate partaking of the Holy Spirit; i.e., those who benefit by the Holy Spirit's presence in the assembly.

[2]R. C. Trench (*Synonyms of the New Testament* [Grand Rapids: Wm. B. Eerdmans Publishing Company, 1948], 77) describes the distinction between these two words: "The *holokleros* (complete person) is one who has preserved, or who, having once lost, has now regained, his *completeness*: the *teleios* (perfect, mature person) is one who has attained his moral *end*, that for which he was intended, namely, to be a man in Christ; however, it may be true that, having reached this, other and higher ends will open out before him, to have Christ formed in him more and more. In the *holokleros* no grace which ought to be in a Christian man is deficient; in the *teleios* no grace is merely in its weak imperfect beginnings, but all have reached a certain ripeness and maturity."

Sanctification

[3]Most commentators take James 5:14–15 as a reference to physical illness. Daniel R. Hayden ("Calling Elders to Pray" *Bibliotheca Sacra*, 138:258–66) offers a different interpretation. He takes the words "sick" and "restore" as a reference to emotional problems or guilt, a "healing of the heart." The word "heal" (James 5:16) is used in Hebrews 12:12–13 of such healing of the heart, and elders are normally concerned with spiritual problems.

[4]I have no strong objection to saying that theoretically a person could go without sinning if he or she always appropriated God's resources. The trouble with such a view is that it usually goes along with the theory of complete eradication of the flesh (sin nature), a theory that runs into trouble with both Scripture as well as human experience.

[5]The literal meaning, "agree with God about our sin," is based on both the etymology as well as the general use of the Greek *homologeo*, "to say the same thing," hence, "to acknowledge."

[6]It is possible that a kind of sorrow, one leading to repentance and the other failing to produce repentance, is not the issue at all. In his comments on 2 Corinthians 7:10, Murray Harris (*Second Corinthians* in *The Expositor's Bible Commentary*, Vol. 10, [Grand Rapids: Zondervan Publishing House, 1976], 363) says: "Verse 10 describes two ways of reacting to pain or sorrow. God's way ('godly sorrow' or sorrow 'as God intended,' *kata theon*, vv. 9, 10, 11) invariably produces a change of heart, and this repentance 'leads to salvation' and therefore gives no cause for regret. . . . What makes the suffering remedial is not the actual experience of it but the reaction to it. . . ."

[7]The classic work on discipleship, stressing the concept of its commitment, is Dietrich Bonhoeffer's *The Cost of Discipleship* (New York: The Macmillan Company, 1960).

[8]This view can be found in Ryrie's *Balancing the Christian Life*, and in Zane C. Hodges' *The Gospel Under Siege* (Redencion Viva, 1981).

Notes

[9] See Ryrie, *Balancing the Christian Life*, 170.

[10] See Dwight Pentecost, *Design for Discipleship* (Grand Rapids: Zondervan Publishing House, 1971), 14–21.

[11] Ryrie, *Balancing the Christian Life*, 170–73.

[12] See J. Oliver Buswell, *Systematic Theology*, Vol. III (Grand Rapids: Zondervan Publishing House, 1962), 175–86, for his development of the idea of commitment in faith.

[13] See Gary Friesen's (*Decision Making and the Will of God* [Portland, Oregon: Multnomah Press, 1980], 97–115) interpretation of passages like Prov. 3:5–6; Ps. 32:8; Isa. 30:20–21; Col. 1:9; 4:12; Rom. 12:1–2; Eph. 2:10; 5:15–17. Friesen's conclusion is that these merely refer to God's "moral" will, not His "individual" will for each believer. I strongly suspect that American Evangelicalism's concept of the "perfect" will for each believer is a product more of American individualism than of biblical teaching.

Chapter Five

[1] Many translations render the Greek *panoplia* in Eph. 6:11, 13 as "whole armor" or something equivalent, denoting completeness. Markus Barth (*Ephesians*, Vol. 2, 793) proposes the idea of *quality* rather than completeness for a number of reasons.

[2] The New Testament passages about reconciliation never suggest that God was an "enemy" or "against" the sinner. His holy character needed "propitiation" (satisfaction), but He takes the initiative in reconciling sinners to Himself. This factor makes spiritual reconciliation distinct from reconciliation between humans.

[3] See Ps. 13:1; 22:1; 74:1; 88:13–18; and Lam. 3:1–18.

Appendix

[1] Robert M. Anderson, *Vision of the Disinherited* (New York: Oxford University Press, 1979), 289–90.

[2] For a complete historical and theological study see Benjamin B. Warfield, *Perfectionism*, Vols. I–II (London: Oxford University Press, 1931). The best description of Wesley's view can be obtained in "Plain Account of Christian Perfection," *The Works of John Wesley* (Grand Rapids: Baker Book House, 1978). Finney describes his view in *Views of Sanctification* (Wieland Tract Depository, 1877).

[3] Wesley, *Works*, 78–79.

[4] I. Howard Marshall, "Sanctification in the Teaching of John Wesley and John Calvin," *Evangelical Quarterly* 34 (1962): 79.

[5] Such is the language of Charles Finney, *Views of Sanctification*, 16.

[6] Some modern commentators, like I. Howard Marshall (*The Epistles of John* in *The New International Commentary* [Grand Rapids: Wm. B. Eerdmans Publishing Company, 1978], 180) and Glenn Barker (*The Epistles of John* in *The Expositor's Bible Commentary* [Grand Rapids: Zondervan Publishing House, 1982], 331), indeed prefer this "idealistic" view, more from the standpoint of John's approach toward the false teachings behind the writing of these letters than from a belief in possible perfection in this life.

[7] Sources for Keswick teaching are Steven Barabas, *So Great Salvation* (London: Marshall, Morgan and Scott, 1952) and Evan H. Hopkins, *The Law of Liberty in the Spiritual Life* (London: Marshall, Morgan and Scott, 1952).

[8] Barabas, *So Great Salvation*, 115.

[9] Ibid., 107.

[10] Ibid.

[11] J. I. Packer uses this term in "Keswick and Sanctification," *The Evangelical Quarterly* 27 (July, 1955): 161.

[12] Charles Ryrie uses this term in "Contrasting Views on Sanctification," *Walvoord: A Tribute* (Chicago: Moody Press, 1982), 197.

Notes

[13]Sources for the Reformed view are Louis Berkhof, *Systematic Theology* (Grand Rapids: Wm. B. Eerdmans Publishing Company, 1941), 527–44; Benjamin B. Warfield, *Perfectionism*; and Abraham Kuyper, *The Work of the Holy Spirit* (Grand Rapids: Wm. B. Eerdmans Publishing Company, 1941).

[14]Ryrie, "Contrasting Views on Sanctification," *Walvoord: A Tribute*, 195.

[15]Packer, "Keswick and Sanctification," *The Evangelical Quarterly*, 155.

[16]Berkhof, *Systematic Theology*, 534.

[17]Kuyper, *The Work of the Holy Spirit*, 494.

[18]Ibid., 310–14.

[19]Packer, "Keswick and Sanctification," *The Evangelical Quarterly*, 157–67. Pelagianism teaches that the will of the unregenerate person was not affected by the Fall. Biblical commands to the regenerated, however, may imply that their wills are to some extent free to choose good.

[20]See Chafer, *He That Is Spiritual* (Grand Rapids: Zondervan Publishing House, reprinted 1967). Other recent proponents of this view are John Walvoord, Charles Ryrie, and Dwight Pentecost. There is some reason to believe that Chafer's and Moody's views of sanctification were influenced by the writings of John Nelson Darby, according to Arthur K. Robertson, "The New Testament Doctrine of Sanctification as Found in the Published Writings of John Nelson Darby (1800–1882)" (Unpublished Ph.D. dissertation, New York University, 1975; University Microfilms).

[21]See Chafer, *He That Is Spiritual*, 22, 56–58.

[22]Ryrie, *Balancing the Christian Life*, 169–81.

[23]Chafer, *He That Is Spiritual*, 20, 22. See my objection to this exegesis on page 168, footnote.

[24]Ryrie, "Contrasting Views on Sanctification," *Walvoord: A Tribute*, 191.

[25]Ibid., 193–94.

BIBLIOGRAPHY

A. Books

Baldwin, H.A. *Holiness and the Human Element.* Louisville: Pentecostal Publishing Company, 1919.

Barabas, Steven. *So Great Salvation.* London: Marshall, Morgan and Scott, 1952.

Barnhouse, Donald G. *Life by the Son: Practical Lessons in Experimental Holiness.* Philadelphia: Pinebrook Book Clubs, 1939.

_____. *God's Methods for Holy Living.* Philadelphia: Eternity Book Service, 1951.

Baxter, J. Sidlow. *Christian Holiness: Restudied and Restated.* Grand Rapids: Zondervan Publishing House, 1977.

_____. *His Deeper Work in Us: A Further Enquiry into New Testament Teaching on the Subject of Christian Holiness.* Grand Rapids: Zondervan Publishing House, 1974.

_____. *Our High Calling: A Series of Devotional and Practical Studies in the New Testament Doctrine of Sanctification.* Grand Rapids: Zondervan Publishing House, 1976.

Belew, Pascal P. *The Case for Entire Sanctification.* Kansas City: Beacon Hill Press, 1974.

Berkouwer, G.C. *Faith and Sanctification.* Grand Rapids: Wm. B. Eerdmans Publishing Company, 1952.

Bonar, Horatio. *God's Way of Holiness.* Chicago: Moody Press, 1970.

Brengle, Samuel L. *Helps to Holiness.* New York: Salvation Army Printing and Publishing House, 1914.

Bridges, Jerry. *The Pursuit of Holiness.* Colorado Springs: Navpress, 1978.

Brockett, Henry E. *Scriptural Freedom From Sin: A Defense of the Precious Truth of Entire Sanctification by Faith and An Examination of the Doctrine of "The Two Natures."* Kansas City: Beacon Hill Press, 1965.

Brown, Charles Ewing. *The Meaning of Sanctification*. Salem, Ohio: Schmul Publishers, n.d.

Cattell, Everett L. *The Spirit of Holiness*. Grand Rapids: Wm. B. Eerdmans Publishing Company, 1963.

Chafer, Lewis Sperry. *He That Is Spiritual*. Grand Rapids: Zondervan Publishing House, 1976.

Clark, Dougan. *The Theology of Holiness*. Boston: Donald and Gill Company, 1893.

Cook, Thomas. *New Testament Holiness*. London: Charles H. Kelly, 1903.

Crane, J.T. *Holiness: The Birthright of All God's Children*. New York: Nelson Phillips, 1874.

Deal, William S. *The March of Holiness: A Brief History of Holiness Doctrine*. Kansas City: Beacon Hill Press, 1978.

Finney, Charles G. *Sanctification*. Ed. William Ernest Allen. London: Christian Literature Crusade, n.d.

—————. *Views of Sanctification*. Toronto: Willard Tract Depository, 1877.

Fletcher, John W. *Christian Perfection: With a Letter by Thomas Rutherford*. Louisville: Pickett Publishing Company, 1897.

Flew, Robert Newton. *The Idea of Perfection in Christian Theology: An Historical Study of the Christian Ideal for the Present Life*. Oxford: Clarendon Press, 1968.

Forsyth, P.T. *Christian Perfection*. New York: Hodder & Stoughton, n.d.

Foster, Randolph S. *Nature and Blessedness of Christian Purity: With an Introduction by Edmund S. Janes*. New York: Lane and Scott, 1851.

Gritter, George. *The Quest for Holiness: The Development of Spiritual Life*. Grand Rapids: Wm. B. Eerdmans Publishing Company, 1955.

Hegre, Theodore. *The Cross and Sanctification*. Minneapolis: Bethany Fellowship, 1962.

Hopkins, Evan H. *The Law of Liberty in the Spiritual Life*. London: Marshall, Morgan and Scott, 1952.

Bibliography

Ironside, Harry A. *Holiness: The False and the True.* Neptune, New Jersey: Loizeaux Brothers, 1912.

Jessop, Harry Edward. *Foundations of Doctrine in Scripture and Experience: A Student's Handbook on Holiness.* Chicago: The Chicago Evangelistic Institute, 1938.

Keplar, Thomas S. (ed.). *Christian Perfection As Believed and Taught by John Wesley.* Cleveland: World Publishing Company, 1954.

Koberle, Adolf. *The Quest for Holiness: A Biblical, Historical and Systematic Investigation.* Trans. John C. Mattes. Minneapolis: Augsburg Press, 1936.

Kuyper, Abraham. *The Work of the Holy Spirit.* Grand Rapids: Wm. B. Eerdmans Publishing Company, 1956.

La Rondelle, H.K. *Perfection and Perfectionism: A Dogmatic-Ethical Study of Biblical Perfection and Phenomenal Perfection.* Berrien Springs, Michigan: Andrews University Press, 1971.

Law, William. *Christian Perfection.* Ed. E. P. Rudolph. Carol Stream, Illinois: Creation House, 1975.

Liege, Pierre Andre. *What is Christian Life?* Trans. A. Manson. New York: Hawthorn Books, 1961.

Mallalieu, W.F. *The Fullness of the Blessing of the Gospel of Christ.* Cincinnati: Jennings and Pye, 1903.

Marsh, F.E. *The Spiritual Life: Our Helps and Hindrances.* London: Pickering and Inglis, n.d.

McDonald, William. *Scriptural Way of Holiness.* Boston, 1893. No further data due to missing title page.

Needham, David C. *Birthright.* Portland, Oregon: Multnomah Press, 1979.

Neill, Stephen Charles. *Christian Holiness: The Carnahen Lectures for 1958.* London: Lutterworth Press, 1960.

Owen, John. *The Holy Spirit: His Gifts and Power.* Grand Rapids: Kregel Publications, 1954.

Pache, Rene. *The Person and Work of the Holy Spirit.* Chicago: Moody Press, 1954.

Sanctification

Parsons, Martin. *The Call to Holiness: Spirituality in A Secular Age.* Grand Rapids: Wm. B. Eerdmans Publishing Company, 1975.

Paxton, Ruth. *Called Unto Holiness.* London: Marshall, Morgan and Scott, 1936.

Pearse, Mark Guy. *Thoughts on Holiness.* Chicago: The Christian Witness, 1903.

Peck, George. *The Scripture Doctrine of Christian Perfection Stated and Defended: With a Critical and Historical Examination of the Controversy, Ancient and Modern.* New York: Carlton and Porter, 1842.

Pentecost, Dwight. *Designed to be Like Him.* Chicago: Moody Press, 1966.

Peters, John Leland. *Christian Perfection and American Methodism.* New York: Abingdon Press, 1956.

Pink, Arthur W. *The Doctrine of Sanctification.* Swengel, Pa.: Reiner Publications, 1971.

Prior, Kenneth. *The Way of Holiness: A Study in Christian Growth.* Downers Grove, Illinois: InterVarsity Press, 1982.

Purkiser, W.T. *Interpreting Christian Holiness.* Kansas City: Beacon Hill Press, 1971.

Rose, Delbert R. *A Theology of Christian Experience: Interpreting The Historic Wesleyan Message.* Minneapolis: Bethany Fellowship, 1965.

Ryle, J.C. *A Call to Holiness.* Grand Rapids: Baker Book House, 1976.

Ryrie, Charles. *Balancing the Christian Life.* Chicago: Moody Press, 1969.

————. "Contrasting Views of Sanctification," *Walvoord: A Tribute.* Ed. Donald K. Campbell. Chicago: Moody Press, 1982.

Sangster, William Edwin Robert. *The Path to Perfection: An Examination and Restatement of John Wesley's Doctrine of Christian Perfection.* London: Epworth Press, 1957.

Bibliography

Simpson, Albert Benjamin. *The Christ Life*. New York: Christian Alliance Publishing Company, 1925.

Smeaton, George. *The Doctrine of the Holy Spirit*. Swengel, Pa.: Reiner Publications, 1958.

Smith, Wilbur M. *The Word of God and the Life of Holiness*. Grand Rapids: Zondervan Publishing House, 1957.

Treffry, Richard. *A Treatise on Christian Perfection*. Boston: McDonald and Gill, 1888.

Turner, Richard. *The More Excellent Way: The Scriptural Basis of the Wesleyan Message*. Winona Lake, Indiana: Light and Life Press, 1952.

Warfield, Benjamin B. *Perfectionism*. London: Oxford University Press, 1931. 2 vols.

Watson, G.D. *A Holiness Manual*. Chicago: The Christian Witness Company, 1882.

Wesley, John. "Plain Account of Christian Perfectionism" in *The Works of John Wesley*. Grand Rapids: Baker Book House, 1978, (11:366–446).

B. Theologies

Berkhof, Louis. *Systematic Theology*. Grand Rapids: Wm. B. Eerdmans Publishing Company, 1941, 527–44.

Bloesch, Donald D. *Essentials of Evangelical Theology*. San Francisco: Harper & Row, 1978, 2:31–70.

Calvin, John. *Institutes of the Christian Religion*. Ed. John T. McNeill. Trans. Ford Lewis Battles. Philadelphia: The Westminster Press, 1955, 3:3:10–15.

Chafer, Lewis Sperry. *Systematic Theology*. Grand Rapids: Zondervan Publishing House, 1948, 3:355–70.

Hodge, Charles. *Systematic Theology*. New York: Scribner, Armstrong, and Company, 1873, 3:213–58.

Pieper, Francis. *Christian Dogmatics*. St. Louis: Concordia Publishing House, 1953, 3:3–86.

Strong, Augustus H. *Systematic Theology*. Philadelphia: The Judson Press, 1907, 869–81.